Sustainable Finance

Sustainable Finance is a concise and authoritative reference series linking research and practice. It provides reliable concepts and research findings in the ever growing field of sustainable investing and finance, SDG economics and Leadership with the declared commitment to present the theories, methods, tools and investment approaches that can fulfil the United Nations Sustainable Development Goals and the Paris Agreement COP 21/22 alongside with de-risking assets and creating triple purpose solutions that ensure the parity of profit, people and planet through choice architecture passion and performance. The series addresses market failure, systemic risk and reinvents portfolio theory, portfolio engineering as well as behavioural finance, financial mediation, product innovation, shared values, community building, business strategy and innovation, exponential tech and creation of social capital. Sustainable Finance and SDG Economics series helps to understand keynotes on international guidelines, guiding accounting and accountability principles, prototyping new developments in triple bottom line investing, cost benefit analysis, integrated financial first plus impact first concepts and impact measurement. Going beyond adjacent fields (like accounting, marketing, strategy, risk management) it integrates the concept of psychology, innovation, exponential tech, choice architecture, alternative economics, blue economy shared values, professions of the future, leadership, human and community development, team culture, impact, quantitative and qualitative measurement, Harvard Negotiation, mediation and complementary currency design using exponential tech and ledger technology. Books in the series contain latest findings from research, concepts for implementation, as well as best practices and case studies for the finance industry. This book series is indexed in SCOPUS

Karen Wendt • Marta Ra
Editors

Sustainable Wealth Management Revisited

Female Leaders Transforming the Industry

Springer

Editors
Karen Wendt
President Sustainable Finance
Eccos Impact GmbH
Cham, Switzerland

Marta Ra
Cynos AG, Alvicus AG
Women In Sustainable Finance
Zurich, Switzerland

ISSN 2522-8285 ISSN 2522-8293 (electronic)
Sustainable Finance
ISBN 978-3-032-02529-6 ISBN 978-3-032-02530-2 (eBook)
https://doi.org/10.1007/978-3-032-02530-2

This Springer imprint is published by the registered company Springer Nature Switzerland AG
The registered company address is: Gewerbestrasse 11, 6330 Cham, Switzerland

Foreword

Sustainable Wealth Management

In a world facing pressing challenges—climate change, biodiversity loss, pollution, and growing social inequities—managing wealth is no longer just about growth. It is about responsibility, resilience, and impact. By embracing sustainable wealth management, wealth managers and their clients do more than secure financial returns; they become stewards of prosperity, ensuring a thriving future for generations to come. In today's globalized economy, a portfolio is not an isolated collection of assets but an interconnected ecosystem where the externalities of one company become the risks of another. The value of an asset extends beyond its balance sheet, influencing ecosystems, communities, and long-term financial stability; it reverberates across industries and economies, eroding value in ways that traditional financial models often fail to capture. Private wealth managers and ultra-high-net-worth individuals have the capacity to recognize these interdependencies as threats to long-term portfolio stability. Contributing to the fight against climate change and biodiversity loss is essential for wealth preservation across generations, and it is therefore not just an ethical imperative—it is a strategic necessity for protecting wealth in an evolving world.

This book also marks a shift in the voices shaping finance. Written entirely by women, it offers fresh perspectives, bold leadership, and a deep commitment to a more sustainable financial future.The expertise and vision shared here are not just about managing assets—they are about redefining what it means to create lasting value.

Each chapter of this book explores key facets of modern wealth management, from time-tested strategies in long-term and short-term investing to the integration of AI, impact investing, and sustainable finance. It challenges outdated paradigms by examining wealth management through a gender-specific lens, highlighting the growing influence of female investors and the unique opportunities that emerge when inclusivity and innovation drive financial decision-making. With case studies, expert insights, and real-world applications, this book equips readers with the tools to navigate an evolving financial landscape—one where sustainable investing, holistic client engagement, and cutting-edge technologies define success.

At its core, this book delivers a powerful message: wealth is more than numbers—it is a legacy, a force for positive change, and a bridge to the future.

Head Sustainable Finance at WWF Switzerland Amandine Favier
Zurich, Switzerland

Contents

Chapter 1
Introduction

Karen Wendt and Marta Ra

1.1 Introduction

1.1.1 Purpose of the Publication

The financial landscape is undergoing a profound transformation, driven by the increasing influence of female leaders who are reshaping the wealth management industry. As the world moves towards a more inclusive and sustainable economic model, the role of women in wealth management has never been more crucial. *Sustainable Wealth Management: Female Leaders Transforming the Industry* seeks to offer a comprehensive exploration of how female leaders are revolutionizing the wealth management sector, with a keen emphasis on sustainable practices and diverse perspectives. This book aims to deepen the understanding of the growing relevance of ethical wealth management and female leadership roles within the industry.

Readers will uncover how the evolving wealth management landscape presents new challenges and opportunities for female leaders. The book highlights transformative strategies that foster sustainable and inclusive growth, emphasizing the necessity of gender-diverse leadership in wealth management. By incorporating insights into investment planning, risk management, sustainability, and technological advancements, this publication aspires to illuminate the crucial contributions of women in shaping the future of wealth management.

K. Wendt
President Sustainable Finance, Eccos Impact GmbH, Cham, Switzerland
e-mail: karen@sustainablefinance.io

M. Ra (✉)
Women In Sustainable Finance (WISF), Zurich, Switzerland
e-mail: marta.ra@wisfinternational.com

K. Wendt, M. Ra (eds.), *Sustainable Wealth Management Revisited*, Sustainable Finance, https://doi.org/10.1007/978-3-032-02530-2_1

1.1.2 Scope and Objectives

Wealth Management, as stated by (Baki, 2023), offers affluent clients the highest level of tailored financial services with the goal of sustained asset growth in mind. This book offers a comprehensive exploration of how female leadership is transforming the industry, with a strong focus on ethical investment strategies and long-term financial sustainability. It delves into the evolving landscape of wealth management, highlighting both the opportunities and challenges faced by women as they navigate this traditionally male-dominated industry. By examining transformative strategies that promote inclusive growth, we emphasize the necessity of diverse leadership in fostering resilience and innovation within wealth management.

Sustainable wealth management is more than just a financial concept; it is a framework that integrates environmental, social, and governance (ESG) factors into financial planning, investment decision-making, and risk assessment (Nitulescu et al., 2022). By aligning financial goals with ethical and sustainable aspirations, wealth managers can contribute to global well-being while ensuring long-term profitability. Women are at the forefront of this shift, driving sustainable solutions that not only enhance financial returns but also promote social and environmental responsibility (Baki, 2023).

This publication explores key themes central to modern wealth management. It provides an in-depth analysis of sustainable wealth strategies (Baki, 2023), differentiating between asset and wealth management while emphasizing the significance of gender inclusivity. Additionally, it evaluates various wealth management strategies, including long-term and short-term investment approaches, risk-reward balancing, and personalized financial solutions.

Further, this book investigates the changing landscape of wealth management, focusing on how the increasing presence of female clients and a gender-lens approach is reshaping the industry. It also examines the role of technological advancements, such as AI-powered wealth planning and fintech solutions, in the evolving industry (Gorman, 2021).

A major focus is placed on sustainable investing as the new normal in wealth management. ESG investment strategies, regulatory frameworks, and SDG-aligned investments are analyzed to highlight their growing impact (Tamimi & Sebastianelli, 2020). The book also explores impact investing, particularly women investing in women, and includes case studies demonstrating the influence of female investors in driving sustainable financial change.

Moreover, longevity finance, a gender-specific approach, is examined in-depth, addressing financial products and demographic trends related to longevity. The book also delves into AI-driven financial planning, risk management, and client engagement, showcasing how emerging technologies are shaping the future of wealth management.

1.1.3 Importance of Female Representation in Wealth Management: Key Findings

Female subject matter experts play increasingly vital and transformative roles in sustainability accounting in the modern economy (Baki, 2023). They have been the primary agents of transformative change, challenging conventional norms while offering constructive perspectives and gifts to the world. Diverse leadership has addressed the globally inherent skills challenge and is well-poised to meet the global challenges of the next decade (Baki, 2023). Also, diverse leadership enables and supports value creation, supporting efficiency, cost mitigation, innovation and creativity, resilience, and quality decisions, all of which play a crucial role in creating sustainable impact (Gorman, 2021).

Female leadership in wealth management is central to improving sustainability practices and diversifying perspectives on environmental, social, and governance issues (Nitulescu et al., 2022). Women in Leadership initiatives' intersections with sustainability, gender equality, and private sector development support women executives keen on innovative opportunities to amplify their impact on wealth sustainability.

Ultimately, *Sustainable Wealth Management: Female Leaders Transforming the Industry* aims to uncover the untapped potential of women in wealth management, advocating for their increased presence in leadership roles. By doing so, they pave the way for a more equitable, sustainable, and innovative financial future for their clients and the financial industry.

This book serves as both a resource and an inspiration, highlighting the critical role of female leaders in shaping the future of wealth management and driving impactful change in the industry.

References

Baki, N. (2023). Women in wealth management and woman-woman, man classification, diversity alignment. Available at SSRN 4478083. https://papers.ssrn.com/sol3/papers.cfm?abstract_id=4478083.

Gorman, T. S. (2021). The attorney-general as wealth manager: Asset seizure, Financial Management and Surplus Profit Allocation Springer Nature. https://link.springer.com. Doi: https://doi.org/10.1007/978-3-030-61562-6_7.

Nitulescu, A., Vinerean, S., Butu, A.-M., & Monthienvichienchai, L. (2022). ESG equity investment portfolio performance in different business conditions. *Technological and Economic Development of Economy, 28*(7), 1667–1689. https://doi.org/10.3846/tede.2022.18871

Tamimi, E., & Sebastianelli, R. (2020). Empirical study of the quantitative effect of the sustainable development goals on the financial performance of companies. *SAGE Open, 10*(4), 1–8. https://doi.org/10.1177/2158244020962205

Chapter 2
Understanding Sustainable Wealth Management

Natalie Baki

2.1 Wealth with Purpose: A New Perspective

In recent years, sustainable wealth management has emerged as an important approach for individuals and families seeking to align their financial decisions with broader social and environmental goals, ensuring that these decisions also resonate with their personal values. At its core, sustainable wealth management integrates traditional wealth preservation and growth strategies with ethical and responsible investment principles, offering a "wealth with purpose" mindset that goes beyond financial returns. This approach acknowledges that wealth can be a force for positive change when managed with consideration.

The main distinction between traditional and sustainable investing lies in the motivation behind investment decisions. While traditional investing is primarily driven by profitability—focusing solely on generating financial returns—sustainable investing adds a deeper layer to the decision-making process. Investors engaged in sustainable strategies seek not just monetary gain but also investment opportunities that reflect their personal values and contribute to societal or environmental well-being (Baker H K et al., 2022). For example, a sustainable investor may prioritize investments in renewable energy projects over traditional fossil fuels, even if it means slightly lower short-term returns, because it aligns with their commitment to environmental responsibility.

Unlike traditional investors who may be satisfied with balancing risk and return, sustainable investors prioritize broader actions. They seek to make positive environmental and social contributions through their financial choices. These investors increasingly seek tailored products and solutions that align with their values, which stands in contrast to traditional approaches that focus mainly on profit maximization (Baker H K et al., 2022).

N. Baki (✉)
Globalance Bank AG, Zurich, Switzerland

K. Wendt, M. Ra (eds.), *Sustainable Wealth Management Revisited*, Sustainable Finance, https://doi.org/10.1007/978-3-032-02530-2_2

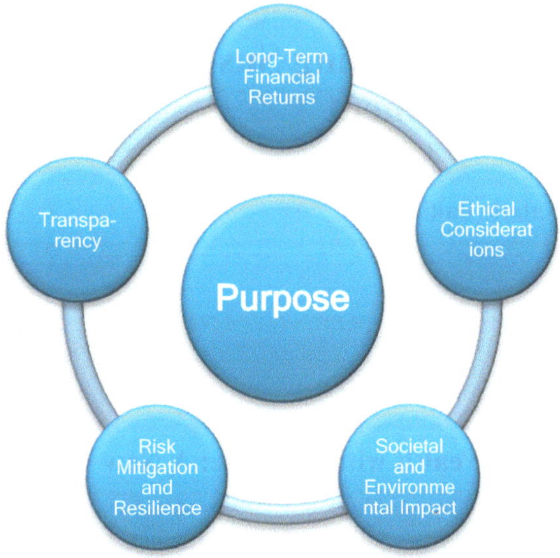

Fig. 2.1 Purpose and its drivers, own representation

As sustainable investing has expanded, it has evolved into a more sophisticated and widely accepted option for many investors. Once considered niche, sustainable investing is gaining mainstream attention as demand grows for investments that deliver both financial returns and societal impact. This approach recognizes that wealth should serve a purpose beyond personal gain, aligning more closely with broader social and environmental objectives. This is what makes sustainable wealth management unique—its ability to integrate both profit and purpose (Baker H K et al., 2022).

The integration of responsible criteria (as shown in Fig. 2.1) into decision-making processes provides investors with new ways to engage with their wealth—ensuring that their capital contributes to a future that is not only financially secure but also socially just and environmentally sound.

While the following are some of the most important considerations, it is important to note that sustainable wealth management encompasses a broader range of factors that continue to evolve as the landscape of responsible investing grows.

Long-Term Financial Returns Financial performance remains an essential aspect of sustainable wealth management, but the approach emphasizes achieving these returns without sacrificing social and environmental integrity. Sustainable investments are viewed as prudent strategies for mitigating risks associated with climate change, resource depletion, and shifting societal expectations.

Ethical Considerations Beyond financial results, sustainable wealth management integrates values-based decision-making. Ethical criteria—such as labor rights, corporate governance, and community development—play a central role in determining which investments are pursued. These factors resonate with a growing number of investors seeking alignment between their wealth and personal beliefs.

Societal and Environmental Impact Sustainable wealth management seeks to create positive societal and environmental impact alongside financial returns. It promotes investments that contribute to a low-carbon economy, foster inclusivity, or support innovation in healthcare, education, and sustainable agriculture.

Risk Mitigation and Resilience Integrating sustainability factors into financial strategies also serves as a robust risk mitigation tool. Companies and sectors that operate unsustainably may face increasing regulatory pressure and are more exposed to reputational risks. Therefore, sustainable wealth management proactively seeks to build resilient investment portfolios by investing in industries and companies that are well-positioned to thrive in a future shaped by sustainability imperatives.

Transparency Transparency is a vital component of sustainable wealth management, ensuring that investors are provided with clear and comprehensive information regarding their investments. Regular and detailed reporting on the social, environmental, and financial impacts of the investments enables investors to track their portfolio's performance and alignment with sustainability goals. For instance, transparency could mean that investors receive specific data on the CO2 emissions associated with their portfolio, allowing them to see how their investments impact the environment. This transparency fosters trust and allows investors to make informed decisions, ensuring that their wealth is managed in line with their values and long-term objectives.

The rise of sustainable wealth management reflects the growing awareness among investors of the urgent global challenges we face, from climate change to social inequality. Increasingly, individuals and families recognize that their financial decisions carry profound implications for the world around them. Wealth management, in this context, is no longer just a tool for personal financial security, but also a vehicle for contributing to the well-being of society and the environment.

2.2 Strategic Balance: Asset vs Wealth Management

In the world of financial planning, both asset management and wealth management play important roles, but they serve distinct purposes and cater to different client needs.

2.2.1 Defining Asset Management

Asset management is centered on managing and growing financial assets, including stocks, bonds, real assets and alternative investments. Its main goal is to help clients achieve optimal returns by making well-informed investment choices, often focusing on particular asset classes or sectors. The process relies on strategies like portfolio optimization, risk control, and diversification to enhance client wealth while minimizing exposure to risk (Corporate Finance Institute, 2024).

Asset management typically caters to large institutional investors like pension funds and endowments, focusing on short to medium-term financial returns. Asset managers generally measure their success through financial metrics and industry benchmarks, reflecting their results-oriented approach and strong emphasis on delivering solid financial outcomes (Corporate Finance Institute, 2024).

2.2.2 *Defining Wealth Management*

In contrast to asset management, wealth management offers a more inclusive and comprehensive approach. It involves not only investment decisions but also services such as tax planning, estate planning, retirement planning, and risk management. Wealth management focuses on both the growth of financial assets and the protection and transfer of wealth to future generations (Ernst & Young, 2021).

This service is highly tailored to the specific needs of wealthy individuals or families with more complex financial situations. Its goal is to design long-term strategies that reflect a client's personal objectives and values, with an increasing focus on sustainability. Wealthy individuals, in particular, are placing great importance on ensuring that their wealth contributes positively to society and the environment. This client-focused approach looks beyond just financial returns, aiming for the long-term stability of wealth while factoring in ethical and responsible considerations (Ernst & Young, 2021).

2.2.3 *Legacy and Impact*

While asset and wealth management prioritize financial growth, many individuals and families are increasingly focused on leaving a legacy, where their wealth contributes positively to society. They aim for their wealth to have a positive impact on the environment and society, both today and for future generations. While these goals echo philanthropic aspirations, it is important to clarify that within the context of this chapter, the focus remains on achieving financial profitability. The intent is not purely charitable; instead, it involves strategically aligning investments with values that contribute to social and environmental progress, all while ensuring capital growth or capital preservation.

2.3 Sustainable Wealth: Shaping the Future of Investing

There are many frameworks within sustainable wealth management, all of which offer nuanced perspectives on sustainability. Sustainable wealth management is a multi-faceted concept that integrates various criteria aimed at balancing financial returns with ethical and environmental considerations.

Below is a list of the most known and common ones (Fig. 2.2) used in wealth management. It is important to recognize that these criteria often overlap and interconnect. Furthermore, there are additional criteria and methodologies beyond those listed below.

Environmental, Social, and Governance (ESG) Investing ESG refers to a set of criteria used by investors and fund managers to evaluate companies based on their environmental impact, corporate governance practices, and social responsibility. ESG investing emerged from a 2004 report by The Global Compact, which stressed the role of large financial institutions in improving corporate management quality by addressing these factors. Companies that perform well on ESG issues can enhance shareholder value through proactive risk management, regulatory adaptation, and market expansion opportunities. ESG investing is not just about social purpose; it's a smart investment strategy that helps to minimize risk. It aims to generate competitive financial returns by focusing on companies that perform well on

Fig. 2.2 Sustainable investment frameworks, own representation

environmental, social, and governance criteria. Many mutual funds and Exchanged Traded Funds (ETFs) incorporate ESG criteria in their investment process (Hill J, 2020).

Socially Responsible Investment (SRI) SRI is an ethical investment strategy that excludes companies or industries based on specific values, such as those involved in alcohol, tobacco, gambling, firearms, or human rights violations. It often uses a "negative screen" to divest from undesirable businesses. In addition to exclusion, SRI can also involve actively investing in companies that promote social justice, environmental solutions, or provide valuable services to communities. Unlike ESG investing, which focuses on including companies based on positive performance across environmental, social, and governance factors, SRI emphasizes ethical exclusion (Hill J, 2020).

Sustainable Development Goals (SDGs) The SDGs are a set of 17 global objectives established by the United Nations, aimed at tackling issues like poverty, inequality, climate change, and environmental degradation by 2030. These goals encompass areas such as health, education, sustainable economic growth, and responsible consumption, promoting collaboration among governments, businesses, and civil society (United Nations, 2024).

Financial investments can align with these goals by directing capital toward projects and companies that contribute to sustainable development and positive social and environmental outcomes. However, accurately measuring an investment's true alignment with the SDGs can be challenging, given the complexity and broad scope of these goals.

Impact Investing Impact investing is a strategy that aims to generate both positive social or environmental impacts and financial returns. It goes beyond traditional investing by intentionally targeting projects or companies that address pressing global issues, such as renewable energy, access to healthcare and education, while still seeking financial gain. Impact investing is proactive, directing capital to solutions that drive measurable, positive change. Investors actively manage these investments to ensure that their financial goals align with their impact objectives, and they rely on standardized metrics to measure outcomes (Rockefeller Philanthropy Advisors, 2024).

Thematic Investing Thematic investing is an investment strategy that focuses on capitalizing on long-term trends such as technological innovation, climate change, or demographic shifts, rather than traditional sector-based strategies. It identifies and groups companies based on these overarching themes, aiming to provide exposure to structural shifts that are expected to shape the global economy over time (Bérubé V et al., 2014).

Corporate Engagement and Shareholder Advocacy Corporate engagement and shareholder advocacy involve investors actively influencing the behavior of companies they invest in by exercising their rights as shareholders. This can include direct dialogue with company management, filing shareholder proposals, or voting on key issues such as environmental policies, social responsibility, or corporate governance. The goal is to encourage companies to improve their practices, leading to enhanced performance, which can mitigate risks and improve long-term financial returns. Unlike passive investment strategies, shareholder advocacy directly pushes for change within companies, ensuring that investors' values are reflected in corporate decision-making (Barko T et al., 2022).

Carbon Footprint and Climate Risk Metrics Carbon footprinting refers to the process of measuring the greenhouse gas (GHG) emissions that a portfolio finances. This metric helps investors understand their exposure to climate-related risks, particularly from high-carbon industries. Key metrics such as financed emissions and financed-emissions intensity allow for assessing the total emissions a portfolio is responsible for. While other metrics like production-based intensity or weighted average carbon intensity help evaluate exposure to carbon-intensive sectors. These metrics guide investors in aligning their investments with decarbonization objectives and managing transition risks related to climate change (MSCI, 2024).

A powerful aspect of sustainable wealth management is that investors can actively direct their capital towards a sustainable purpose. By doing so, they support investments that prioritize sustainability or have a positive impact on society and the environment. At the same time, investors have the opportunity to withdraw or divest from investments that are not aligned with sustainability goals or have a negative impact.

Sustainable investing is a tool that can be used to address key global challenges, such as reducing climate risk, fostering inclusion, and promoting long-term positive change. It enables investors to align their financial goals with their values, ensuring that their wealth contributes to a better future for both current and future generations. By embracing this approach, investors can harness the power of their capital not only for financial growth but also to help shape a more sustainable and equitable world.

2.4 Women Leading the Change in Wealth Management

The wealth management industry is undergoing a significant transformation, driven by an increasing number of female leaders and clients who are reshaping the landscape with a focus on sustainability, inclusivity, and long-term value creation. This growing influence of women in wealth management is not only changing how wealth is managed, but also reshaping investment priorities to emphasize sustainable practices and social responsibility. As both clients and leaders, women are at the forefront of this shift, creating a more forward-thinking and inclusive approach to wealth management.

2.4.1 Women as Wealth Holders and Clients

Women's financial influence is expanding significantly. The BCG Global Wealth Report has shown that women control around 32% of the world's wealth, this figure is from 2019 and is expected to rise even further in the coming years (Boston Consulting Group, 2020).

This increase not only represents growing numbers but also a shift in priorities. More women are using their wealth to contribute to societal well-being, opting for investments that reflect their values, especially in areas like sustainability and social equality (UBS, 2021).

For example, research shows that 71% of British women strive to live more ethically, compared to 59% of men (Mintel, 2018). This trend is mirrored in investment behaviors, with female clients increasingly prioritizing long-term sustainability over short-term financial gains. This alignment of personal values with financial decisions is a growing force in the wealth management industry, driving significant changes in how wealth managers approach their role as advisors (Mintel, 2018). As the financial influence of women continues to grow, it is not only shaping investment behaviors but also driving changes in leadership across the industry.

2.4.2 Women as Leaders in Wealth Management

Women are increasingly taking on leadership roles within the wealth management industry, challenging traditional norms in male-dominated fields. Their approach to wealth management brings a broader and more inclusive perspective, focusing on both financial success and sustainability (UBS, 2021).

As Christine Lagarde, President of the European Central Bank, has pointed out, empowering women is critical not only for fairness and diversity but also for economic growth and inclusivity (Lagarde C, 2019).

Female-led companies have been particularly resilient, especially during crises like the COVID-19 pandemic, where women leaders excelled in crisis management. Their qualities—such as empathy, collaboration, and a long-term perspective—are key to advancing sustainability in wealth management (UBS, 2021). Moreover, a 2018 study by Warwick Business School found that women outperformed men in investment returns by 1.8% per year. This outperformance can be attributed to women's tendency to adopt a longer-term investment perspective and trade less frequently. This approach suggests that women are more focused on achieving their financial goals, while men may be more drawn to the excitement of frequent trading (Warwick Business School, 2018).

Research also indicates that women are more likely than men to invest in social and climate impact initiatives, often selecting investments that align with their values. Increasing women's participation in investment could therefore add an estimated $1.87 trillion to sustainable investments, which could have a broader positive impact on society and the planet (BNY Mellon, 2021).

2.4.3 *Women Leaders Driving Sustainability and Inclusivity*

Women are leading the way in the ESG movement, championing responsible investing practices. In the U.S., women are increasingly driving demand for ESG investments, which is consistent with their focus on using wealth for positive social and environmental impact. Female investors are more likely than men to consider long-term societal and environmental outcomes, positioning them as key drivers of the shift towards sustainable wealth management (RBC Wealth Management, 2021).

The increasing presence of women in leadership roles within financial institutions is shaping corporate cultures and strategies. These female leaders are advocating for policies that emphasize ESG factors, working to embed these principles into the core of their firms' investment approaches. This evolution is pushing wealth management toward more ethical, responsible, and sustainable practices (RBC Wealth Management, 2021).

2.4.4 *Creating a More Inclusive Approach*

The rising influence of women in wealth management is also fostering a more inclusive industry. By focusing on long-term sustainability and inclusive growth, female leaders are challenging traditional models of wealth management that prioritize profit above all else. Instead, they are advocating for strategies that balance financial returns with social responsibility. This approach not only benefits individual investors but also contributes to broader societal goals, such as reducing inequality and promoting environmental sustainability (UBS, 2021).

As a result, women are increasingly being seen not only as wealth holders and clients but also as key decision-makers who are shaping the future of the financial industry. Their leadership is helping to create a more forward-thinking and inclusive approach to managing wealth—one that aligns financial success with positive social impact (UBS, 2021).

References

Books

Baker, H. K., Holzhauer, H. M., & Nofsinger, J. R. (2022). *Sustainable investing: What everyone needs to know*. Oxford University Press.

Barko, T., Cremers, M., & Renneboog, L. (2022). Shareholder engagement on environmental, social, and governance performance. *Journal of Business Ethics*.

Bérubé, V., Ghai, S., & Tétrault, J. (2014). *From indexes to insights: The rise of thematic investing*. McKinsey Invest.

Hill, J. (2020). Environmental, Social, and Governance (ESG) investing: A balanced analysis of the theory and practice of a sustainable portfolio.

Online Documents

BNY Mellon. (2021). The pathway to inclusive investment https://www.bnymellonim.com/content/dam/imemea/static-html-files/The-Pathway-to-Inclusive-Investment/asset/bnym_im_allstreet_report_en_apac_optimised.pdf Accessed October 3, 2024.
Boston Consulting Group. (2020). Managing the Next decade of women's wealth. https://www.bcg.com/publications/2020/managing-next-decade-women-wealth. Accessed September 27, 2024.
Corporate Finance Institute. (2024). Asset management vs. wealth management: What's the difference?, https://corporatefinanceinstitute.com/resources/career/asset-management-vs-wealth-management/. Accessed September 26, 2024.
Ernst & Young. (2021). How wealth managers can help clients live their values now, https://www.ey.com/en_gl/insights/wealth-asset-management/how-wealth-managers-can-help-clients-live-their-values-now. Accessed September 26, 2024.
Lagarde C. (2019). A global imperative. https://www.linkedin.com/pulse/global-imperative-christine-lagarde. Accessed September 27, 2024.
Mintel. (2018). The eco gender gap: 71% of women try to live more ethically, compared to 59% of men. https://www.mintel.com/press-centre/the-eco-gender-gap-71-of-women-try-to-live-more-ethically-compared-to-59-of-men/. Accessed September 27, 2024.
MSCI. (2024). Carbon footprinting demystified. https://www.msci.com/documents/10199/a57d8424-34a9-3ea4-5a74-030349845bb3. Accessed September 26, 2024.
RBC Wealth Management. (2021). Women are leading the charge for Environmental, Social and Governance (ESG) investing in the U.S. amid growing demand for responsible investing solutions, https://www.rbcwealthmanagement.com/en-us/newsroom/2021-04-06/women-are-leading-the-charge-for-environmental-social-and-governance-esg-investing-in-the-us-amid-growing-demand-for-responsible-investing-solutions. Accessed September 27, 2024.
Rockefeller Phliantrophy Advisors. https://www.rockpa.org/guide/impact-investing-introduction/. Accessed September 26, 2024.
UBS. (2021). Women's wealth 2030. https://www.ubs.com/global/en/wealth-management/women/2021/women-wealth-parity-power-purpose/_jcr_content/mainpar/toplevelgrid/col2/teaser/linklist/actionbutton.0808140295.file/PS9jb250ZW50L2RhbS9hc3NldHMvd20vZ2xvYmFsL2RvYy93b21lbi13ZWFsdGgtcmVwb3J0LTIwMzAucGRm/women-wealth-report-2030.pdf. Accessed September 27, 2024.
United Nations. (2024). https://sdgs.un.org/goals. Accessed September 26, 2024.
Warwick Business School. (2018). Are women better investors than men? https://www.wbs.ac.uk/news/are-women-better-investors-than-men/. Accessed October 3, 2024.

Chapter 3
Wealth Management Strategies

Sabrina Failo

3.1 Long-Term Investment Planning

This part focuses on developing long-term investment plans that align with clients' financial goals. It emphasizes the importance of strategic asset allocation, diversification, as well as the power of compounding to drive consistent growth. The integration of sustainable factors such as ESG principles can further enhance portfolio resilience and meet the increasing demand for responsible investing.

Wealth management is a comprehensive financial service that provides clients with tailored investment advice, financial planning, and asset management to meet their long-term financial goals. It involves a holistic approach, integrating various aspects of financial management such as retirement planning, tax optimization, estate planning, and risk management. The goal of wealth management is to preserve and grow wealth while addressing the client's unique financial needs. (The Research Foundation of CFA Institute, 2010).

The rise of wealth management practices can be attributed to the growing complexity of financial markets and the increasing need for personalized financial strategies. As individuals' wealth has grown, particularly among high-net-worth individuals (HNWIs), the demand for professional advice has surged (Capgemini Research Institute, 2024). Wealth management services evolved to provide clients bespoke solutions and more sophisticated investment strategies. Additionally, advancements in technology, financial products, and global markets have further fueled the growth of wealth management as a critical service in managing and protecting wealth across generations.

S. Failo (✉)
Women in Sustainable Finance (WISF), Zurich, Switzerland
e-mail: sabrina.failo@wisfinternational.com

K. Wendt, M. Ra (eds.), *Sustainable Wealth Management Revisited*, Sustainable Finance, https://doi.org/10.1007/978-3-032-02530-2_3

3.1.1 Strategic Asset Allocation: The Foundation of Long-Term Planning

Strategic Asset Allocation (SAA) is a key component of long-term investment planning, as it involves determining the optimal balance of the different asset classes such as equities, bonds, real estate, and alternative investments, based on a client's constraints. Through this approach an investment advisor can establish a long-term framework which is consistently adapted to the client's needs evolving over time.

The Strategic Asset Allocation (SAA) results from an analysis combining a client's Investment Policy Statement (IPS) with current market conditions. Using various investment tools, a manager can identify the most suitable portfolio that meets the client's preferences by selecting it from the range of efficient portfolios. The IPS is a formal document created after analyzing the client's investment objectives and constraints, including factors like risk tolerance, time horizon, liquidity needs, and tax considerations. The IPS plays a critical role in portfolio management; when regularly updated and adapted, it ensures that both the client and advisor are working toward the same financial objectives. The goal of SAA is to balance risk and return by allocating investments across diverse asset classes. For example, equities typically offer higher growth potential but imply greater volatility, and therefore by definition higher risk, making them more suitable for long-term horizons. On the other hand, bonds historically provided more stability and income, making them more adapt to clients seeking consistent returns with lower risk. Generally, real estate and alternative investments, such as private equity, can add further diversification and reduce overall portfolio volatility at the cost of lower liquidity.

Periodic rebalancing is essential in strategic asset allocation, since market fluctuations may cause certain asset classes to deviate from their target weights, increasing risk exposure or diluting returns. Rebalancing ensures the portfolio remains aligned with the client's original objectives, maintaining the intended balance between growth and security.

3.1.2 Diversification: Reducing Risk Through Broad Exposure

Diversification is a fundamental principle in long-term investment planning, as it reduces unsystematic risk by allocating investments across various sectors, industries, geographies, and asset classes. A well-diversified portfolio ensures that poor performance in one area is offset by stronger performance in another, helping to stabilize returns over time (Bodie et al., 2005).

Global diversification, for instance, allows investors to benefit from growth opportunities in both developed and emerging markets while mitigating risks associated with specific economies. Sectoral diversification, on the other hand, ensures exposure to a range of industries, from technology and healthcare to utilities and consumer goods. Including alternative investments, such as commodities or infrastructure, can further enhance diversification, providing a hedge against inflation and other economic uncertainties.

Diversification not only protects against downside risk but also enables investors to capitalize on a broader range of opportunities, ensuring steady growth over the long term.

3.1.3 *The Power of Compounding: Growth Over Time*

Compounding is a critical factor in long-term investment planning; indeed, it allows investments to grow exponentially over time. Compounding occurs when the returns generated by an investment are reinvested, earning additional returns in subsequent periods (Bodie et al., 2005). "Time in the market" is one of the pillars of compounding and highlights the importance of starting early and remaining consistently invested. For example, Fig. 3.1 illustrates that an initial \$10,000 investment earning an average annual return of 7% would grow to only \$31,000 over 30 years without the reinvestment the returns. On the other hand, reinvesting the returns over the same period would increase the investment's value to \$76,000. This highlights the power of compounding and how long-term investors are rewarded for maintaining consistency and patience, even during market volatility.

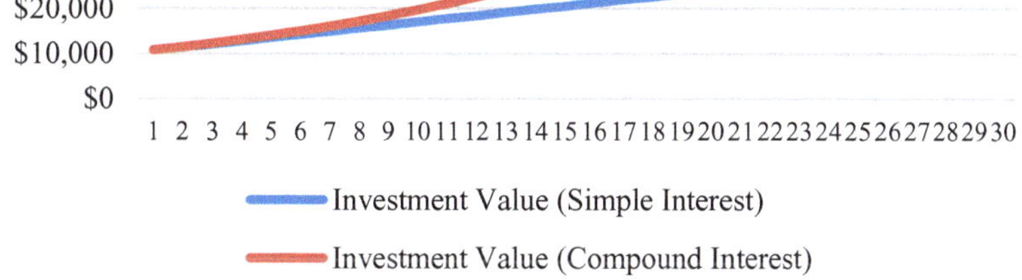

Fig. 3.1 Power of compounding: growth of the investment value with and without return reinvestment over a 30 year period assuming an average annual return of 7% (own illustration)

3.1.4 Integrating ESG Principles for Sustainable Growth

Incorporating sustainability principles into long-term investment planning has become increasingly important, as clients demand portfolios that align with their values while delivering financial returns (Morgan Stanley, 2024). ESG investing involves selecting companies or assets that meet specific environmental, social, and governance criteria, ensuring that investments contribute positively to society and the environment.

For instance, an ESG-aligned portfolio might prioritize renewable energy companies, businesses with strong labor practices, or firms with diverse and inclusive leadership. These investments not only address the ethical concerns of clients but also offer potential financial advantages, as companies with strong ESG practices are often better positioned to manage risks and capitalize on opportunities in the changing economic landscape.

Studies have shown that ESG-focused investments can provide comparable returns to traditional investments, particularly in the long term (Friede et al., 2015). By integrating ESG factors into strategic asset allocation and security selection, investors can achieve resilience and growth while supporting sustainability.

Overall, long-term investment planning requires a thoughtful, disciplined approach that aligns with the client's financial aspirations. By leveraging strategic asset allocation, diversification, and compounding, wealth managers can build portfolios that deliver consistent growth while managing risk effectively. Integrating sustainable factors like ESG principles enhances the portfolio's resilience and aligns with the values of modern investors.

A proactive and client-focused strategy not only helps achieve financial goals but also positions clients to withstand market volatility and adapt to an evolving investment landscape. With the right long-term plan, investors can confidently navigate their financial journeys while contributing to a more sustainable future.

3.2 Short-Term Investment Approaches

This section examines short-term strategies aimed at identifying market trends and seizing opportunities, while effectively managing volatility and liquidity. It discusses how Tactical Asset Allocations (TAA) approaches can be implemented to balance the need for short-term returns with the broader goals of sustainable investing.

3.2.1 Tactical Asset Allocation: A Flexible Approach

Tactical asset allocation is a cornerstone of short-term strategies, allowing investors to adjust their portfolios dynamically to capitalize on immediate market opportunities. Unlike strategic asset allocation, which focuses on long-term stability, tactical approaches involve temporary deviations from the standard allocation to respond to emerging trends or anticipated market shifts. For example, if a particular industry, such as clean energy, is expected to experience rapid short-term growth due to regulatory changes, an investor might temporarily overweight that sector. Tactical allocation provides the flexibility to take advantage of such opportunities, but it also requires a disciplined approach to avoid overreacting to market noise or making poorly timed decisions.

3.2.2 Managing Volatility and Liquidity

Short-term investing inherently involves navigating market volatility. Strategies in this category often aim to mitigate risks associated with sharp price movements while maintaining sufficient liquidity to adapt to changing conditions. Effective management of volatility ensures that investors can avoid large drawdowns, while liquidity provides the ability to act quickly when opportunities arise. Liquid assets such as exchange-traded funds (ETFs), money market instruments, or highly traded stocks are commonly used in short-term strategies. These instruments allow for quick transactions without significant price impact, ensuring that investors can move in and out of positions efficiently.

3.2.3 Balancing Short-Term Returns with Broader Goals

While the primary objective of short-term strategies is to achieve quick returns, it is crucial to align these efforts with broader investment goals. This is particularly true in sustainable investing; while short-term strategies can target sustainable opportunities with immediate positive impacts, such as short-term green bonds or sustainable infrastructure projects, the biggest impact is achieved through a consistent and long-term approach. By ensuring that short-term strategies are not only focused on immediate profits but also consider broader environmental, social, and governance factors, investors can create a more integrated and impactful investment approach. This balance between short-term returns and long-term objectives ultimately supports financial success while contributing to global sustainability efforts.

Overall, short-term strategies offer the advantage of flexibility and responsiveness, but they come with inherent challenges. Higher transaction costs, increased exposure to market timing risks, and the potential for emotional decision-making can undermine returns if not managed carefully. Additionally, short-term investors must balance the pursuit of quick gains with the risk of losing sight of their overall financial objectives. Integrating sustainability into short-term strategies adds another layer of complexity, as aligning short-term opportunities with ESG goals requires careful research and monitoring. Success in this area depends on selecting the right tools, maintaining discipline, and ensuring alignment with broader investment plans.

In conclusion, short-term investment strategies provide a dynamic approach to seizing market opportunities and managing liquidity while addressing immediate financial goals. Tactical asset allocation, combined with effective volatility and risk management, allows investors to adapt to changing conditions without losing sight of broader objectives. When aligned with sustainability principles, short-term strategies can complement long-term investments by delivering both financial returns and positive societal impact. By balancing flexibility with discipline, investors can maximize the potential of short-term investing within a comprehensive wealth management framework.

3.3 Balancing Risk and Rewards

This section explores the critical task of balancing risk and reward in portfolio management. It emphasizes the importance of effective risk management in achieving financial goals while considering non-financial factors, such as ESG risks. By incorporating a disciplined approach to risk assessment and mitigation, investors can build resilient portfolios capable of withstanding market fluctuations and delivering long-term returns.

The risk-reward tradeoff is a fundamental concept in investment management. Higher potential returns often come with increased risk, while lower-risk investments typically yield more modest returns. Striking the right balance between these two factors depends on the investor's financial goals, risk tolerance, and time horizon. For instance, younger investors with a longer time horizon may tolerate higher risk to pursue greater returns, investing in equities or growth-focused assets. Conversely, retirees or those with shorter time horizons may prioritize capital preservation through safer, income-generating investments like bonds. Understanding this tradeoff ensures that portfolios are aligned with client objectives while managing potential downsides.

3.4 Risk Management: Building Resilient Portfolios

Effective risk management is essential for building portfolios that can weather market volatility and deliver consistent performance over time. This involves identifying, measuring, and mitigating risks across all levels of the portfolio, from individual assets to overall allocation. Diversification is one of the most powerful tools for risk management. By spreading investments across asset classes, sectors, and geographies, investors can reduce exposure to the underperformance of any single area. For example, combining equities with bonds or real estate provides a buffer against market downturns, as these asset classes often behave differently under similar conditions. Additionally, tools like stop-loss orders, hedging strategies, and stress testing help mitigate risks. Stress testing, in particular, allows investors to evaluate how portfolios might perform under adverse scenarios, such as economic recessions or geopolitical instability, enabling proactive adjustments to enhance resilience.

3.5 Tools for Balancing Risk and Reward

Several tools and strategies are essential for achieving an optimal balance between risk and reward:

- Risk Profiling: Assessing an investor's risk tolerance helps tailor the portfolio to their comfort level, ensuring alignment with financial goals. The IPS is a convenient tool allowing to understand the risk appetite of the client as well as all constraints and needs. Risk budgeting is a practice that further contributes to managing the risks by setting an overall risk limit that is permitted within the SAA, TAA and security selection.
- Strategic Asset Allocation: Setting a long-term allocation framework balances growth and stability while minimizing unnecessary risks, and ensuring they are frequently revisited to adapt to evolving client circumstances.
- Dynamic Rebalancing: Periodically adjusting the portfolio to maintain target allocations and respond to market changes.
- Active Monitoring: Continuously evaluating the performance and risk of individual assets and the overall portfolio ensures timely adjustments.

These tools collectively support disciplined decision-making, helping investors navigate the complexities of market dynamics while achieving sustainable growth.

3.6 Core-Satellite Approach

The core-satellite approach is an investment strategy designed to balance risk and reward by combining the stability of a core portfolio with the flexibility of satellite investments. The core, typically comprising 70–90% of the portfolio, consists of low-cost, broadly diversified investments such as index funds or ETFs. This portion provides a stable foundation, aligning with long-term objectives and ensuring consistent, market-like returns. The satellite portion, making up 10–30% of the portfolio, includes higher-risk or specialized investments, such as sector-specific funds, alternative assets, or actively managed strategies. These satellite investments aim to enhance returns, capitalize on niche opportunities, or align with specific themes like

ESG goals. By maintaining a diversified core to mitigate risks while using satellites to pursue higher returns, the core-satellite approach effectively balances reliability and growth potential. This strategy is particularly appealing for its flexibility, cost efficiency, and ability to adapt to evolving market conditions and investor preferences.

3.7 Incorporating ESG Risks in Portfolio Management

Incorporating ESG risks into portfolio management is increasingly important in today's investment landscape, adding an additional layer of risk management. ESG factors, such as climate change, labor practices, and corporate governance, can significantly impact the long-term performance and stability of investments. Companies with poor environmental practices may face regulatory fines, reputational damage, or declining market relevance, leading to financial losses. Conversely, firms with strong ESG credentials are often better positioned to manage risks and capitalize on emerging opportunities, making them attractive long-term investments. Nevertheless, investors must also carefully consider the risk of greenwashing, where companies or investment products misrepresent their ESG credentials to appear more sustainable than they truly are. Greenwashing can expose portfolios to hidden risks, as investments believed to align with sustainability principles may fail to meet standards, resulting in reputational harm and underperformance. To mitigate this, investors should rely on robust ESG data, conduct thorough due diligence, and evaluate third-party ratings critically, recognizing their potential limitations and biases.

By integrating ESG considerations into the risk management process while being vigilant against greenwashing, investors can align their portfolios with sustainable practices and mitigate non-financial risks that could impact performance. This dual focus enhances portfolio resilience and supports the growing demand for authentic responsible investing, ensuring both ethical and financial integrity.

Resilient portfolios are those that can withstand short-term market fluctuations without compromising long-term objectives. By focusing on diversification, strategic asset allocation, and ESG integration, investors can create portfolios that deliver consistent returns while adapting to changing market conditions. For example, during periods of heightened volatility, maintaining a diversified portfolio with exposure to less-correlated asset classes, such as bonds or infrastructure, can help reduce drawdowns. Similarly, actively incorporating ESG factors ensures that investments are future-proofed against evolving regulatory and market trends.

In conclusion, balancing risk and reward in portfolio management is a dynamic process that requires careful consideration of both financial and non-financial factors. By adopting robust risk management practices, integrating ESG considerations, and leveraging diversification, investors can build resilient portfolios that meet their long-term goals. This approach not only safeguards against market volatility but also positions investors to capitalize on opportunities, ensuring sustainable and consistent performance in an ever-changing investment landscape.

3.8 Personalized Wealth Management Solutions

This section emphasizes the importance of creating tailored wealth management strategies that address the unique needs, values, and goals of each client. By considering individual preferences and objectives, personalized approaches ensure that every aspect of the financial plan aligns with the client's priorities. This client-centric method fosters trust, enhances satisfaction, and enables better financial outcomes.

Personalized wealth management begins with a deep understanding of the client's financial goals, risk tolerance, and values. Clients may prioritize objectives like retirement planning, education funding, or philanthropy, while others may focus on aligning their investments with ethical or sustainability principles. By recognizing these priorities, wealth managers can craft financial plans that reflect not only the client's financial needs but also their personal beliefs and aspirations. For example, a client passionate about environmental issues might prioritize ESG-compliant investments, while another seeking intergenerational wealth transfer may require strategies focused on estate planning and legacy preservation. Understanding these nuances ensures the financial plan is not just functional but meaningful to the client.

3.8.1 Investment Policy Statement

The Investment Policy Statement (IPS) CFA Institute (2010) is a framework through which an investment manager collects a wide set of information to understand the clients' needs and develop a personalized wealth management strategy. The IPS is a formal document setting all investment constraints and guidelines as well as information on benchmarks to evaluate performance. Ultimately the major components of an IPS address the following key factors:

- Financial Situation: Assessing the client's current assets, liabilities, income, and expenses forms the foundation of the plan.
- Risk Tolerance: Understanding how much risk a client is willing and able to take ensures the investment strategy is appropriate.
- Time Horizon: Long-term goals like retirement may require different strategies than short-term goals like buying a home.
- Values and Preferences: Incorporating clients' preferences, such as a focus on sustainability or sector-specific investments, adds a personal touch to the plan.
- Tax and Legal Considerations: Tailoring strategies to optimize tax efficiency and adhere to legal requirements ensures financial security.

By considering these factors, wealth managers can design comprehensive, client-focused plans that address all aspects of the client's financial life.

3.8.2 Leveraging Technology for Personalization

In recent years wealth managers have increased investments in technology to boost productivity and reallocate advisor efforts toward growth-focused tasks, reflecting a shift in priorities to drive value and client satisfaction (McKinsey & Company, 2024). In general, advances in technology have significantly enhanced the ability to deliver personalized wealth management solutions. Tools like robo-advisors, AI-driven analytics, and client-facing financial planning platforms enable wealth managers to gain deeper insights into client behavior, preferences, and financial goals. For instance, AI can analyze historical data to anticipate client needs or recommend tailored investment strategies based on individual risk tolerance and objectives. Digital platforms further enhance transparency, allowing clients to monitor and adjust their portfolios in real-time, fostering greater engagement and trust. These technologies also make personalization scalable, ensuring that even clients with smaller portfolios receive tailored attention.

3.8.3 Benefits of Personalized Wealth Management

Tailored strategies offer several key advantages to wealth advisors, among which:

- Stronger Client Relationships: By aligning strategies with personal values and goals, wealth managers build deeper trust and long-term relationships with clients.
- Improved Financial Outcomes: Individualized plans are more likely to address specific needs, ensuring better results over time.
- Adaptability: Personalized solutions can evolve with the client's changing circumstances, maintaining relevance and effectiveness.
- Higher Engagement: Clients feel more involved and invested in financial plans that reflect their unique preferences.

Personalized wealth management is a powerful approach that aligns financial plans with the unique inclinations of each client. By understanding individual needs, leveraging advanced technology, and incorporating ESG considerations, wealth managers can create tailored solutions that foster trust and deliver meaningful outcomes. This client-centric focus not only ensures financial success but also empowers clients to achieve their broader aspirations, making their wealth management journey both impactful and fulfilling.

3.9 Conclusions

Wealth management strategies encompass a holistic and dynamic approach to achieving financial success, blending long-term planning, short-term adaptability, effective risk management, and personalization. By leveraging strategic asset allocation, diversification, and the power of compounding, long-term strategies provide stability and consistent growth. Short-term strategies complement this foundation by capturing immediate opportunities and managing liquidity and volatility, aligning these efforts with broader financial and sustainable goals.

Balancing risk and reward is fundamental to building resilient portfolios, with tools like diversification, ESG integration, and risk assessment ensuring long-term stability. Personalized wealth management solutions further enhance the client experience by tailoring strategies to individual needs, fostering trust and stronger client relationships. Technology serves as a key enabler across these strategies, improving efficiency, scalability, and alignment with modern investment demands.

Together, these strategies provide a comprehensive framework that not only meets clients' financial aspirations but also adapts to the complexities of an evolving market landscape. With the right combination of approaches, wealth managers can help clients achieve their goals while contributing to a more sustainable financial future.

References

Bodie, Z., Kane, A., & Marcus, A. (2005). *Investments* (6th ed.). McGraw-Hill.

Capgemini Research Institute. (2024). Intelligent strategies for winning with the ultra-wealthy. Available at https://www.capgemini.com/insights/research-library/world-wealth-report/. Accessed November 22, 2024.

CFA Institute. (2010). Elements of an investment policy statement for individual investors. Available at: https://rpc.cfainstitute.org/-/media/documents/article/position-paper/investment-policy-statement-individual-investors.pdf. Accessed November 22, 2024.

Friede, G., Busch, T., & Bassen, A. (2015). ESG and financial performance: Aggregated evidence from more than 2000 empirical studies. Available at https://www.tandfonline.com. https://doi.org/10.1080/20430795.2015.1118917.

McKinsey & Company. (2024). US Wealth management: Amid market turbulence, an industry converges. Available at https://www.mckinsey.com/industries/financial-services/our-insights/us-wealth-management-amid-market-turbulence-an-industry-converges#/. Accessed November 18, 2024.

Morgan, S. (2024). Sustainable signals understanding individual investors' interests and priorities. Available at: https://www.morganstanley.com/content/dam/msdotcom/en/assets/pdfs/MSInstituteforSustainableInvesting-SustainableSignals-Individuals-2024.pdf. Accessed November 18, 2024.

The Research Foundation of CFA Institute. (2010). Private wealth management a review. Available at: https://rpc.cfainstitute.org/-/media/documents/book/rf-lit-review/2010/rflr-v5-n1-1-pdf.pdf. Accessed November 18, 2024.

Chapter 4
Changing Landscape of Wealth Management: The Upcoming Generation of Clients Is More Diverse

Désirée Dosch, Marta Ra, and Barbara Schreier

4.1 The Great Wealth Transfer

The term "The Great Wealth Transfer" refers to the imminent massive transfer of wealth from the baby boomer generation to younger generations, particularly Generation X and millennials. In the US, it is estimated that around USD 84 trillion will be transferred by 2045, with around USD 16 trillion expected to be transferred in the next 10 years (Standard Chartered, 2023). A similar picture is emerging in Europe, where significant assets are also passed on between generations. This transfer harbours both opportunities and challenges, particularly regarding the management and preservation of family wealth across generations (MoneyToday, 2020).

The wealth management industry is undergoing a significant transformation, driven by a new generation of clients who are more diverse in terms of demographics, values, and expectations. This shift necessitates that wealth managers adapt their strategies to effectively meet the evolving needs of their clientele (Deloitte, n.d.). The combination of longer life expectancy, professional success, changing family structures and the imminent generational change in wealth will ensure that women will hold a larger share of global wealth in the future (Boston Consulting Group, 2020). The emergence of Millennials and Generation Z as primary wealth holders introduces a client base that is more ethnically diverse and gender-inclusive than previous generations (Deloitte, 2024, Morgan Stanley, 2024, Financial Planning, 2024).

D. Dosch · M. Ra (✉) · B. Schreier
Cynos AG, Alvicus AG, Women in Sustainable Finance (WISF), Zurich, Switzerland
e-mail: desiree@alvicus.com; marta.ra@wisfinternational.cok; schreierkraus@cynos.ch

K. Wendt, M. Ra (eds.), *Sustainable Wealth Management Revisited*, Sustainable Finance, https://doi.org/10.1007/978-3-032-02530-2_4

4.1.1 Transfer of Assets to Women

Over the next few decades, a significant transfer of wealth will take place in which women will play a central role. It is estimated that women will own around two thirds of all wealth in the US by 2030. This change will be supported by the longer life expectancy of women and the increase in female professionals and entrepreneurs (McKinsey & Company, 2020a). On average, women are living longer than men, which means that they are more likely to assume primary responsibility for family wealth. This demographic trend means that women are more likely to inherit and manage assets (Centers for Disease Control and Prevention [CDC], 2021). Many women will inherit significant wealth from parents and partners in the coming decades, as a large distribution of wealth between generations is imminent. This development, known as the "Great Wealth Transfer", will benefit women in particular (Cerulli Associates, 2020). Divorce and other family changes mean that many women gain control over financial assets. As divorce rates remain high worldwide, women are increasingly taking on financial responsibility and managing assets independently (Pew Research Centre, 2019). Changing social role models and increased financial education mean that women are increasingly able to take responsibility for their own finances and make decisions about large assets (UBS, 2020).

In recent decades, women have increasingly embarked on educational and career paths that lead to higher incomes and wealth accumulation. More and more women are taking on highly paid management positions and are increasingly active in entrepreneurial roles (McKinsey & Company, 2020b).

4.1.2 Millennials and Generation Z

The growing financial influence of Millennials and Generation Z as wealth holders signifies a shift in the demographic landscape, with these generations representing a client base that is not only ethnically and culturally diverse but also characterised by a stronger emphasis on gender inclusivity. Unlike their predecessors, these groups are more likely to prioritise values-driven investment strategies, demand equitable representation across all sectors, and advocate for inclusive financial services that cater to a wider range of cultural and gender identities (Deloitte, 2024; EY, 2020; Inyova, 2021; Investopedia, 2022). This diversification reflects broader societal trends towards inclusivity and underscores the need for wealth managers to adapt their approaches to meet the unique preferences and expectations of these younger, socially conscious investors (Pew Research Centre, 2019). According to Deloitte (2023), these generations prioritise equity, inclusion, and sustainability in their financial decisions. This diversification challenges wealth managers to adopt personalised approaches that cater to varying cultural and social contexts. Younger clients are increasingly driven by values such as environmental, social, and governance (ESG) considerations. A report (McKinsey & Company, 2021b) highlights that ESG investments have become a cornerstone for this demographic, as they seek to align their financial portfolios with personal values.

The digital fluency of these generations has accelerated the adoption of technology in wealth management. They expect seamless digital experiences, including AI-driven personalised advice, mobile-friendly platforms, and instant access to financial insights (Ernst & Young, 2022c). When given a choice between a generic advisor and someone who specializes in their exact life stage, neighborhood, demographic, or job industry, clients are more likely to choose someone who can offer hyper-personalised service and understands their unique situation and financial goals (Precisefp, n.d.).

Modern clients demand tailored services that address their unique financial goals. Another report emphasizes that wealth managers must pivot to a client-centric model, focusing on personalisation and holistic financial planning to remain competitive (Capgemini, 2023).

4.2 What Does This Change Mean for the Financial Industry?

4.2.1 Preference for Sustainable and Social Investments

Women attach greater importance to ESG (environmental, social and governance) investments. Studies show that 84% of women attach importance to social or environmental aspects when investing, compared to 67% of men (Morgan Stanley, 2019). According to another study, women tend to place more value on long-term goals and sustainable, responsible asset development. This is linked to the desire to achieve stable and positive returns over a longer period of time, which is reflected in a higher interest in ESG investments (Boston Consulting Group, 2020). Women often have a stronger connection and empathy with social and environmental causes, particularly in areas such as healthcare, education and environmental protection. This personal connection can lead to a greater willingness to invest in ESG-focused projects that have a positive impact on these areas (Fidelity Charitable, 2017).

In addition, sustainability and environmental aspects will become increasingly important for wealth management firms as HNWIs become more sensitive to the ESG impact of their investments. Capgemini's World Wealth Report 2024 (Capgemini, 2024) states that 63% of HNWIs demand reliable and comprehensible ESG assessments for their assets. Firms need to bridge the gap between client demands and organisational capabilities to leverage ESG investing, despite over 30% of relationship managers stating that their firm lacks a standard framework for measuring and assessing ESG impact.

4.2.2 *Asset Management Companies Strategically Integrate Social Aspects*

Asset management firms are strategically leveraging social equity and inclusion to drive better business outcomes. They are increasingly focused on creating, measuring and communicating these issues to meet the needs of socially conscious clients (Capgemini, 2024). While investors are demanding data and tools to measure impact, asset management firms are working to build a more diverse workforce and meet regulatory requirements.

The wealth management industry is making progress towards a more diverse workforce. The number of women and Certified Financial Planners (CFPs) from different ethnic backgrounds is growing (Think Advisor, 2023) Greater diversity can help firms improve their results and serve a more diverse and younger client base.

Asset management companies are promoting social impact through education, mentoring and networking for minorities and underserved groups, by providing capital to entrepreneurs from diverse backgrounds and by investing in critical infrastructure for underserved communities. The following examples illustrate this trend: "Invest in My Education" education and support for disadvantaged students (Business Wire, 2023), establishment of centers offering financial coaching (Wells Fargo, 2022), financial education and career guidance for youth from diverse backgrounds (Morgan Stanley, 2023), investment in early-stage businesses whose founders are women or members of diverse communities (Morgan Stanley, 2021), access to credit and capital for underserved small business owners (Bizwomen, 2023), support for black women-owned businesses (Holland, 2023).

4.2.3 *Reliable and Comprehensible ESG Key Figures*

ESG ratings and metrics will become increasingly important in the coming years as investors continue to diversify their portfolios. In addition to investors' portfolios, asset management companies will also use standardised ESG metrics to measure and mitigate ESG-specific risks in their investments and financial exposures. Readily available ESG metrics will also enable asset managers to offer highly customised ESG-related funds and expand their portfolio of offerings (Boston Consulting Group, 2019; Deloitte, 2019b; Deloitte, 2020; Deloitte, 2021; Ernst & Young, 2020b; KPMG, 2022; McKinsey & Company, 2021a; MSCI, n.d.-a, n.d.-b).

The non-profit Global Impact Investor Network (GIIN) announced a three-year Impact Lab programme to develop analytical benchmarking tools for impact investing (Field, 2022). The program offers investors a data management platform with integrated standard metrics.

The EU has introduced more than a dozen ESG regulations, including the Sustainable Finance Disclosure Regulation and the Corporate Sustainability

Reporting Directive. They also provide information for investors to understand the sustainability impact of the companies they invest in. Harmonised reporting standards, such as the European Sustainability Reporting Standards (ESRS) (European Commission, 2023) in the EU, and initiatives such as the Sustainable Finance Disclosure Regulation (SFDR) (European Commission, n.d.) improve the transparency and comparability of ESG data. These measures strengthen investors' confidence in the proper implementation and effectiveness of ESG investments, as they receive reliable information for making informed decisions.

4.2.4 Growing Demand for Personalisation and Individual Advice

Personalisation and individual advice are very important for Generation Z and millennials, as well as for women.

Generation Z and millennials prefer financial advice that is specifically tailored to their personal life goals, values and financial priorities. They expect wealth managers to cater to their individual needs rather than offering standardised products and generic solutions. These groups value a customised approach that takes into account aspects such as retirement planning, ethical investing and flexible lifestyles (Capgemini, 2023; Deloitte, 2023; Ernst & Young, 2020a; McKinsey & Company, 2022b). Modern technologies such as artificial intelligence (AI) and big data play a crucial role in this, as they enable wealth managers to analyse customer preferences more precisely and make tailored recommendations. Studies show that 72% of millennials expect personalised services and are willing to pay a premium for tailored advice (PwC, 2021).

Women often favour a different approach to wealth management that is more focused on advice and comprehensive financial life planning. They place particular emphasis on personalised and long-term strategies that reflect their life goals and values (Boston Consulting Group, 2020). Women often have different financial priorities and challenges than men, such as longer lifespans, interrupted careers (e.g. due to childcare) and potentially lower pensions. Personalised advice can help to better take these individual needs into account and develop tailored strategies for asset protection and retirement planning (Boston Consulting Group, 2020). Women often value comprehensive financial planning that not only maximises returns, but also considers long-term goals, security and quality of life. They seek advice that combines financial decisions with personal values and life goals (McKinsey & Company, 2020a). Studies show that women often value personal relationships and trust when it comes to financial advice. They prefer advisors who build long-term partnerships and are willing to respond to their unique circumstances rather than just focusing on quick profits (Merrill Lynch Wealth Management, 2018).

4.2.5 Integrative Work Culture in the Financial Sector

Despite their growing influence, women remain underrepresented in the financial services industry, particularly in leadership positions. This lack of diversity could be an obstacle for the industry to understand and fulfil the needs of the next generation of female investors (Oliver Wyman, 2020). This can be attributed to various structural and cultural reasons:

The financial sector is traditionally male-dominated and often has a culture that excludes women or makes it difficult for them to advance. This "old boys' club" mentality often means that women are given fewer opportunities for leadership roles and find themselves in a less supportive working environment (Oliver Wyman, 2020). In many financial organisations, there are few female managers, which means that women lack role models and mentors to support and inspire them. Without such mentors, women often find it harder to network and take advantage of career opportunities (Boston Consulting Group, 2017). The financial sector is known for long working hours and a lack of flexibility, which penalizes women who often have more family commitments. As a result, many women leave the industry or higher positions to find a better work-life balance (McKinsey & Company & LeanIn.Org, 2020). Women in the financial sector are often confronted with prejudices that question their abilities and decision-making power. These stereotypes can lead to women being less respected and less likely to be given the opportunity to prove themselves in positions of responsibility (Coffman et al., 2018). In many financial companies, there is a lack of programs and guidelines that actively promote women and break down gender barriers. Without such measures, access to management levels for women is often severely restricted (Deloitte, 2019a).

The underrepresentation of women in the financial sector is the result of cultural barriers, a lack of role models, a lack of flexibility and persistent prejudices. By taking targeted measures to promote women and create a more inclusive working culture, financial organizations could counteract this trend and bring more women into management positions.

The underrepresentation of women in the financial industry can have a significant impact on customer service. Research shows that diverse teams, especially those with a higher proportion of women, tend to have a better understanding of the needs of a diverse client base and can offer innovative solutions. A lack of female leaders can therefore lead to a one-sided perspective that may not adequately address all customer needs ((Eagly & Carli, 2007, Roth, 2006). With the increase in female heirs and investors, their influence on investment decisions is also growing. Many women are in favour of greater diversity and inclusion in companies and prefer investment managers who value these factors (UBS, 2020).

Generation Z and millennials favour companies that promote an inclusive corporate culture and make diversity visible in their management and advisory teams. This includes ethnic and gender diversity as well as the representation of different perspectives and backgrounds (Smith & Turner, 2015). These generations demand that financial service providers make an authentic commitment to diversity and inclusion and take transparent measures to promote these values (Ernst & Young, 2022a). An inclusive work culture is not only a customer retention tool, but also a strategic advantage in attracting and retaining young talent in the industry. Millennials and Generation Z are looking for employers who share their values and actively embrace inclusion (Deloitte, 2023).

4.2.6 *Digitalisation and Technology Affinity*

Generations Z and millennials are having a significant impact on the wealth management industry. Both generations have grown up with digital technologies and therefore expect seamless digital experiences from financial service providers. This includes mobile applications, online platforms and the use of artificial intelligence for personalized financial advice (EY, 2020, Netcetera, n.d.). Companies that do not fulfil these digital expectations risk losing these customer groups.

How new technologies support Next Gen Wealth Management is explained in Sect. 4.5.

4.3 Measures to Maintain Competitiveness

To remain competitive in the evolving landscape of wealth management, firms must take deliberate steps to address the needs and preferences of a new generation of clients.

First, building culturally sensitive and inclusive teams is essential. Clients, particularly Millennials and Generation Z, expect their financial advisors to understand and reflect their diverse backgrounds and values (Smith & Turner, 2015). An inclusive approach fosters trust and strengthens relationships, ensuring that wealth management firms remain relevant in a multicultural society.

Second, investing in digital solutions is no longer optional but a necessity. With tech-savvy clients demanding seamless and efficient financial services, firms must integrate advanced technologies such as AI-driven personalisation, mobile-friendly platforms, and real-time financial insights. These tools enhance the client experience, increase engagement, and position firms as forward-thinking leaders in the industry (Ernst & Young, 2022b, McKinsey & Company, 2022a).

Lastly, developing clear and transparent ESG metrics is critical to aligning with the values-driven investment preferences of younger clients. Millennials and Generation Z increasingly prioritise sustainability and social impact when making financial decisions. By incorporating robust ESG frameworks, firms can meet these expectations, attract socially conscious investors, and differentiate themselves in a competitive market (Global Impact Investing Network [GI-IN], 2020; Morgan Stanley, 2019).

By embracing inclusivity, digital transformation, and ESG integration, wealth management firms can position themselves as adaptive, innovative, and client-focused, ensuring long-term success in a rapidly changing industry (Capgemini, 2023, Deloitte, 2023).

4.4 Is There a Female Lens into Wealth Management?

4.4.1 Exploring Wealth Management Through a Female Lens: Insights and Strategies

The landscape of wealth management is witnessing a remarkable transformation, with women controlling 38% of $34 trillion in U.S. investment assets, according to McKinsey (2020) findings. Whilst some women view wealth as a cornerstone of security and autonomy, others see it as a catalyst for meaningful societal impact. Let's delve into the unique challenges and opportunities women encounter in managing wealth.

4.4.2 Behavioural Finance

Investment Behaviour

Women tend to embrace a thoughtful, measured approach to wealth planning, with a keen focus on disciplined strategies and log-term objectives. Recent findings from the Spectrem Group reveal that 61% of women seek professional guidance for investment decisions, compared to 56% of men, resulting in 0.4% higher yearly portfolio returns (InvestmentNews, 2021; Fidelity Investments, 2021). Whilst some research suggests men might achieve higher short-term gains due to their higher risk tolerance and more aggressive tactics, women's steady, measured approaches and risk-adjusted strategies often prove more rewarding over time, showcasing their talent for building robust portfolios.

Notable investment characteristics among women include:

A strong interest in environmentally conscious investments

Extended holding periods for financial assets

A tendency to seek professional expertise in decision-making

4.4.3 Risk Tolerance

The common perception of women as risk-averse requires a more nuanced examination. Research indicates that whilst women generally opt for more conservative financial portfolios, financial literacy plays a crucial role in narrowing the gender gap in risk-taking behaviours (Edin & Selin, 2020). Women's emphasis on risk-adjusted returns contributes to greater portfolio stability over time, supported by their disciplined investment approach and longer holding periods. Moreover, women are less likely to engage in 'overtrading', a behaviour that typically limits returns, thus enhancing their portfolio performance (InvestmentNews, 2021).

4.4.4 Portfolio Strategies: Goals and Alignment

Goal-Oriented Planning

Women prioritise personal objectives over market outperformance. According to EY's 2020 research, 40% of affluent women focus on achieving personal goals such as financial independence and sustainability, compared to 34% of men. Conversely, 37% of men prioritise market outperformance, highlighting a distinct difference in investment philosophies. Women's goal-oriented planning typically encompasses:

Establishing clear financial objectives

Synchronising investments with life milestones

Maintaining a long-term outlook

This approach reflects a broader understanding that successful wealth management extends beyond just market performance to encompass personal values and life aspirations.

These nuances underscore how women's financial approaches often harmonise with personal values and long-term vision, contrasting with men's inclination towards higher-risk, performance-centric strategies. Wealth managers must tailor their offerings to effectively address these distinct priorities.

4.4.5 Asset Allocation and ESG Preferences

Portfolio returns are predominantly influenced by strategic asset allocation, accounting for roughly 90% of variability over time, making it a cornerstone of enduring portfolio success (Ibbotson & Kaplan, 2000; HSBC Private Banking, 2023). Women frequently gravitate towards tangible investments like property whilst showing growing enthusiasm for ESG-aligned opportunities, demonstrating their dedication to sustainable wealth building. The Morgan Stanley Institute for Sustainable Investing (2019) reveals that 85% of individual investors show keen interest in sustainable investing, with women displaying marginally higher engagement than men, pointing to a diminishing gender divide in sustainable investment interest. Looking at generational trends, Millennials (born 1981–1996) are spearheading the sustainable investing movement, with 95% showing interest, followed closely by Gen Z (born 1997–2012) at 85%, highlighting younger generations' growing desire to align financial choices with values and sustainability. Moreover, impact investing continues to gain momentum, with 27% of impact investors channelling 30% or more of their assets into women-owned or women-led ventures, according to the Global Impact Investing Network (GIIN, 2024), showcasing the rising prominence of gender lens investing within impact investing circles.

4.4.6 Exploring Alternative Investments

Private Equity and Venture Capital

Whilst women's representation in venture capital leadership remains modest, accounting for roughly 15% of general partners in European venture capital firms (Sifted Research, 2023), increasing gender diversity within these organisations correlates with improved financial outcomes. Studies show that venture capital firms that boosted their female partner appointments by 10% witnessed an average 1.5% yearly increase in fund returns and achieved 9.7% more profitable exits (World Economic Forum, 2023). Female-led startups perform on par with male-led ventures, occasionally surpassing them. Research by the Boston Consulting Group revealed that startups with at least one female founder generated 78 pence in revenue per pound invested, compared to 31 pence for male-led startups (BCG, 2018). This underscores the considerable potential of female-led ventures to drive innovation and create value, particularly in sectors like technology, healthcare, and sustainability.

4.4.7 Building Wealth: Scaling and Sustainability

Women's wealth creation is not only gaining momentum but becoming increasingly sustainable as they adopt strategies that balance growth with long-term resilience. Here's a detailed exploration of the drivers, supported by facts and insights:

Scaling Through Entrepreneurship: Women-owned enterprises are experiencing remarkable growth, sparking innovation and generating employment worldwide. Fresh data from Kilsah Consulting (2023) highlights that women entrepreneurs inject £2.1 trillion annually into the global marketplace. What's particularly striking is that female-led ventures are expanding 4.5 times more rapidly than their male-owned counterparts, demonstrating their keen eye for spotting and maximising market opportunities.

Diversified Income Streams: Women are embracing varied wealth-building approaches to ensure sustainable growth. Recent findings from She Markets Her (2024) spotlight several key strategies:

Real Estate Investments: Women are tapping into property portfolios and REITs to establish steady passive income streams.

Dividend-Paying Stocks: Strategic investments in dividend-yielding shares provide reliable returns whilst maintaining capital growth.

Digital Ventures: Creating and monetising digital assets, from virtual learning programmes to downloadable content, enables scalable revenue with minimal operational costs.

Through their focus on scalability and sustainability, women are transforming the economic landscape. Their business ventures and investment choices yield both substantial financial returns and meaningful societal impact, crafting a path towards a more balanced and thriving future.

4.4.8 Practical Strategies for Wealth Managers

To meet the growing demand for personalized and value-driven wealth management services, wealth managers are encouraged to implement comprehensive strategies that address the unique needs of a diverse group of wealth owners. The following figure illustrates a strategic approach to wealth management.

Tailored Solutions: Wealth managers need to understand the systemic, cultural, and societal factors that influence investors' financial needs. Women, for example, often have longer life expectancies and greater caregiving responsibilities, which can significantly impact their financial situations. By offering personalized services that address these challenges, wealth managers can build strong, lasting relationships with women investors, supporting their financial success while driving long-term growth for the firm.

Personalised Financial Education: Wealth managers should offer financial education programs that cover various life stages, from early career to retirement planning, ensuring that all clients are equipped with the knowledge they need to make informed decisions.

Diverse Teams: Building diverse teams with strong female representation benefits the company both internally and externally. A balanced gender mix not only reduces unconscious biases and strengthens corporate culture within the organization but also enhances service quality by providing a deeper understanding of clients' needs, ultimately leading to greater success for the company.

ESG-Focused Portfolios: Incorporating Environmental, Social, and Governance (ESG) criteria into investment portfolios is increasingly important to a variety of investors. Wealth managers must provide diverse portfolio options that align with clients' desire to generate meaningful impact through their investments.

Community Platforms: Wealth allocation goes beyond finances; it includes networks and relationships. Creating communities and circles where investors can meet, exchange ideas, learn, and grow is essential for fostering a supportive environment that encourages long-term relationships, successful asset allocation, and impactful growth.

4.4.9 Conclusion

Women are revolutionising wealth management through their methodical, purpose-driven approach and commitment to sustainability. Financial institutions can build lasting relationships by meeting these evolving needs. As women's economic influence expands, they continue to reshape the financial sphere, transforming wealth into a catalyst for growth, security, and positive change.

4.5 New Technologies Support Next-Generation Wealth Management

4.5.1 Introduction

Technology is revolutionizing the financial industry, particularly the wealth management industry. This is caused by the game-changers AI (artificial intelligence), the introduction of decentralized finance (DeFi) and fintech in general. Those technological innovations are mainly building male-dominated datasets and product designs and therefore reinforce gender biases. Yet to date female investors are frequently underserved by digital wealth management tools, due to the simple fact that AI models are built on historical financial data primarily reflecting male financial behaviour (Chen et al., 2022). This chapter explores the intersection of technology, gender biases, and the future of inclusive wealth management.

4.5.2 Bias in AI-Driven Wealth Management

To date, there is no gender inclusive data collection, and no algorithmic transparency. As previously mentioned, most datasets predominantly reflect male financial habits which AI-driven financial tools feed on. One research suggests that AI-powered robo-advisors default to risk-taking strategies mostly align with stereotypically male investment patterns. The same research claims this systemic default sidelines women's long-term financial planning needs (Miller & Johnson, 2023). However, the author claims that not all women have as mentioned previously "long term financial needs", nor all men have "short term financial needs" and suggests refraining from generalising investment strategies and preferences simply through gender.

Also, credit scoring models tend to disadvantage women due to their historical underrepresentation in high-income financial activities (Demirgüç-Kunt et al., 2021). Research found that biased AI algorithms of financial services institutions have led to discriminatory lending practices. This resulted in female clients receiving lower credit limits than male clients with similar financial profiles (Bartlett et al., 2021). Those biases need to be overcome, and they require gender-inclusive data collection, as well as algorithmic transparency.

4.5.3 The Role of Fintech's in Bridging the Gender Gap

Unfortunately, many planforms remain unintentionally male-oriented, leaving the potential of fintech to democratize wealth management untapped. Research illustrates that frequently wealth management apps offer functionalities such as aggressive investment strategies or day trading, which often do not serve many of female investors' needs for long-term financial security, claims Ghosh et al. (2022). However, some fintech solution providers are aware of this bias and have identified it as a business opportunity. By offering goal-based investing tailored to women's financial journeys (e.g. maternity breaks and caregiving responsibilities), they aim to close this gap. Pioneers like Ellevest and Wealthsimple are gender-smart wealth platforms which cater to these gender specific needs.

4.5.4 Future of Wealth Advisory: AI and Personalization

Current AI models mostly cannot differentiate gendered financial behaviours, although AI has the potential to deliver hyper-personalized wealth advisory services. Research suggests that female investors are more likely to prioritize sustainable financial planning and impact investing. However, the current offerings for AI-driven tools seldomly optimize portfolios with gender specific goals in mind (Smith et al., 2023). Financial service providers such as banks or wealth managers using AI-based wealth advisors, have to make sure to serve a diverse clientele. This requires the integration inclusive datasets and the development of adaptive algorithms that reflect a variety of financial behaviours.

4.5.5 Blockchain, Decentralized Finance (DeFi), and Inclusion

It is imperative for DeFi platforms to be user-friendly and accessible, ensuring that women can fully participate in the digital financial ecosystem. By fostering inclusivity in DeFi, there is an opportunity to bridge the gender gap in financial services and empower women economically (Ra, 2023).

Blockchain technology and DeFi have democratized access to capital globally, simultaneously creating opportunities within the wealth management sector. Unfortunately, women still remain underrepresented in those sectors of financial services offerings. The Global Blockchain Council surveyed that only 13% of cryptocurrency investors are women, illustrating the gender gap for digital asset ownership (Jones et al., 2022). However, there is a potential for blockchain-based financial products, such as smart contracts or tokenized real estate. This technology could reduce traditional financial gatekeeping barriers while offering more inclusive investment opportunities.

4.5.6 Wealth Tech Work for Women

Financial services providers must consciously and actively integrate gender-inclusive principles into their wealth technology and products to truly cater to all investors. Actions are necessary on various fronts such developing financial tools that accommodate varied financial goals, ensuring diverse datasets, and hiring more women in fintech leadership roles (McKinsey & Company, 2023). Policies need to be established while, at the same time, guidelines are imperative to promote transparency and fairness. Those are all necessary as AI-driven wealth management needs to prevent gender-based financial exclusion. Therefore, ethical AI frameworks and regulatory oversight are essential to mitigate those risks and build trust in digital wealth management solutions.

The future of wealth management depends on the intersection of technology and inclusivity. While AI, fintech, and DeFi offer transformative possibilities, they must be designed with gender-aware frameworks to ensure that all investors, regardless of gender, benefit equally. It is not only a business necessity but also a moral imperative for financial services providers to acknowledge preferences and financial behaviours of female clients. All stakeholders must work collaboratively, through addressing biases in AI algorithms, promoting gender-diverse fintech innovation, and implementing regulatory safeguards; only then the wealth management industry can create a more equitable financial future.

References

Abouzahr, K., Taplett, F. B., Krentz, M., & Harthorne, J. (2018, June 6). Why women-owned startups are a better bet. Boston Consulting Group.

Bartlett, R., Morse, A., Stanton, R., & Wallace, N. (2021). Consumer-lending discrimination in the FinTech era. *Journal of Financial Economics, 141*(1), 1–23.

Bizwomen. (2023, June 28). Wells Fargo supports Hello Alice fund to help underserved small businesses get capital. https://www.bizjournals.com/bizwomen.

Boston Consulting Group. (2017). Bridging the gender gap in finance. Retrieved from https://www.bcg.com/publications/2017/bridging-the-gender-gap-in-finance.

Boston Consulting Group. (2019). How asset managers can seize the lead in sustainable investing. Retrieved from https://www.bcg.com/publications/2019/asset-managers-seize-lead-sustainable-investing.

Boston Consulting Group. (2020). Managing the next decade of women's wealth. Retrieved from https://www.bcg.com/publications/2020/managing-next-decade-women-wealth.

Boston Consulting Group. (2023). Women entrepreneurs: The investment advantage. Retrieved from https://www.bcg.com/women-entrepreneurs-investment-advantage

Business Wire. (2023, January 17). Fidelity investments launches invest in my education (ME) SM, providing access to education and support to historically underserved students. Retrieved from https://www.businesswire.com/news/home/20230117005086/en/Fidelity-Investments-Launches-Invest-In-My-Education-ME-SM-Providing-Access-to-Education-and-Support-to-Historically-Underserved-Students.

Capgemini. (2023). World wealth report 2023 Retrieved from https://www.capgemini.com.

Capgemini. (2024). Wealth management trends 2024: The client-led revolution. Retrieved from https://www.capgemini.com/ch-en/insights/research-library/wealth-management-top-trends-2024.

Catalyst. (2019). Why diversity and inclusion matter: Quick take. Retrieved from https://www.catalyst.org/research/why-diversity-and-inclusion-matter/

Centers for Disease Control and Prevention (CDC). (2021). National vital statistics reports. Retrieved from https://www.cdc.gov/nchs/products/nvsr.htm.

Cerulli Associates. (2020). *U.S. high-net-worth and ultra-high-net-worth markets 2020: Evolving wealth demographics*. Cerulli Associates.

Chen, L., Chien, S., & Brown, M. (2022). Gender bias in AI-driven financial services: An empirical analysis. *Journal of Financial Technology, 15*(3), 204–220.

Coffman, K. B., Exley, C. L., & Niederle, M. (2018). How gender stereotypes influence emerging careers. *Harvard Business Review*. Retrieved from https://hbr.org/2018/05/how-gender-stereotypes-influence-emerging-careers.

Credit Suisse. (n.d.). Women's investment strategies. Retrieved from https://www.credit-suisse.com/uk/en/private-banking/investing/investing-for-women.html.

Deloitte. (2019a). Advancing women in financial services. Retrieved from https://www2.deloitte.com/us/en/insights/industry/financial-services/women-leaders-financial-services.html.

Deloitte. (2019b). Integrating ESG risk into a risk management framework. Retrieved from https://www.deloitte.com/ie/en/Industries/financial-services/research/esg-risk-management-framework.html.

Deloitte. (2020). ESG investing performance for investment management. Retrieved from https://www2.deloitte.com/us/en/insights/industry/financial-services/esg-investing-performance.html.

Deloitte. (2021). ESG investing and sustainability. Retrieved from https://www2.deloitte.com/us/en/insights/industry/financial-services/esg-investing-and-sustainability.html.

Deloitte. (2023). Deloitte Gen Z and Millennial survey 2023. Retrieved from https://www2.deloitte.com/global/en/pages/about-deloitte/articles/gen-z-millennial-survey.html.

Deloitte. (2024). Deloitte Global 2024 Gen Z and Millennial Survey. Retrieved from https://www2.deloitte.com/us/en/insights/topics/talent/deloitte-gen-z-millennial-survey.html.

Deloitte. (n.d.). Wealth management: Winning transformation strategies. Retrieved from https://www.deloitte.com/ch/en/Industries/financial-services/perspectives/wealth-management-winning-transformation-strategies.html.

Demirgüç-Kunt, A., Klapper, L., Singer, D., & Ansar, S. (2021). The global gender gap in financial inclusion: Trends and insights. World Bank Research Papers.

Eagly, A. H., & Carli, L. L. (2007). *Through the labyrinth: The truth about how women become leaders*. Harvard Business School Press.

Edin, P.-A., & Selin, H. (2020). Gender dynamics in financial risk-taking. Retrieved from https://www.ifau.se/globalassets/pdf/se/2020/wp-2020-16-financial-risk-taking-and-the-gender-wage-gap.pdf.

Ernst & Young. (2020a). How personalization drives customer loyalty in financial services. Retrieved from https://www.ey.com.

Ernst & Young. (2020b). Why data remains the biggest ESG investing challenge for asset managers. Retrieved from https://www.ey.com/en_gl/insights/financial-services/emeia/why-data-remains-the-biggest-esg-investing-challenge-for-asset-managers.

Ernst & Young. (2022a). How can today's millennial investors drive tomorrow's business success? Retrieved from https://www.ey.com/en_us/insights/wealth-asset-management/global-wealth-research-millennial-trends.

Ernst & Young. (2022b). How millennials and Gen Z are reshaping wealth management. Retrieved from https://www.ey.com.

Ernst & Young. (2022c). The future of wealth management for digital natives. Retrieved from https://www.ey.com.

Ernst & Young. (n.d.). Generation Z is transforming retail banking. Retrieved from https://www.ey.com/de_de/industries/banking-capital-markets/die-generation-z-transformiert-das-privatkundengeschaeft.

European Commission. (2023, 31 July). Commission adopts European sustainability reporting standards. Retrieved from https://finance.ec.europa.eu/news/commission-adopts-european-sustainability-reporting-standards-2023-07-31_de.

European Commission. (n.d.). Sustainable Finance Disclosures Regulation (SFDR). Retrieved from https://finance.ec.europa.eu/regulation-and-supervision/financial-services-legislation/implementing-and-delegated-acts/sustainable-finance-disclosures-regulation_en.

EY. (2020). Personalising wealth management for women. Retrieved from https://assets.ey.com/content/dam/ey-sites/ey-com/en_gl/topics/wealth-and-asset-management/wealth-asset-management-pdfs/ey-women-wealth-updated.pdf.

Fidelity Charitable. (2017). Women and giving: The impact of empathy on charitable giving. Retrieved from https://www.fidelitycharitable.org/content/dam/fc-public/docs/insights/2017-women-and-giving.pdf.

Fidelity Investments. (2021). Understanding women investors: 2021 Comprehensive study. Retrieved from https://www.fidelity.com/bin-public/060_www_fidelity_com/documents/about-fidelity/FidelityInvestmentsWomen%26InvestingStudy2021.pdf.

Field, A. (2022), October 25. A 'quantum leap forward' for impact measurement with new benchmarking tools. Forbes. Retrieved from https://www.forbes.com/sites/annefield/2022/10/25/a-quantum-leap-forward-for-impact-measurement-with-new-benchmarking-tools/?sh=7b0e185e62b2.

Financial Planning. (2024, 8 March). Millennial and generation Z wealth is growing quickly, report finds. Retrieved from https://www.financial-planning.com/news/millennial-and-gen-z-wealth-is-growing-quickly-report-finds.

Ghosh, S., Patel, N., & Rao, V. (2022). Wealth management for women: Fintech's role in closing the gender gap. *International Journal of Financial Services, 19*(4), 389–405.

Global Impact Investing Network. (2024). Gender lens investing: Transforming finance in 2024. Retrieved from https://thegiin.org/research/gender-lens-investing-2024

Global Impact Investing Network (GIIN). (2020). State of impact measurement and management practice. Retrieved from https://thegiin.org.

Holland, F. (2023, April 4). Goldman Sachs invests $2 billion in Black women-owned businesses-the first chapter of a bigger plan. CNBC. Retrieved from https://www.cnbc.com/2023/04/04/goldman-sachs-one-million-black-women-announces-first-investment.html.

HSBC Private Banking. (2023). Essential investment guidelines for women: A comprehensive approach. Retrieved from https://www.privatebanking.hsbc.com/wih/investments-insights/women-investment-guidelines/.

Ibbotson, R. G., & Kaplan, P. D. (2000). Asset Allocation: Determining Investment Performance. *Financial Analysts Journal, 56*(1), 26–33. https://www.jstor.org/stable/4480220.

InvestmentNews. (2021). The growing trust: Women and financial advisers. Retrieved from https://www.investmentnews.com/women-advisor-community/women-rely-on-financial-advisers-more-than-men/202962.

Investopedia. (2022, 20 May). Gen Z wants to invest in line with their values, but the economy is making that harder. Retrieved from https://www.investopedia.com/genz-wants-to-invest-in-line-with-their-values-but-the-economy-is-making-that-harder-7568328.

Inyova. (2021). How Millennials and Gen Z are shaking up sustainable investing. Retrieved from https://inyova.ch/en/expertise/millenials-gen-z-and-sustainable-investing/.

Jones, P., White, K., & Roberts, T. (2022). The gender disparity in cryptocurrency investment and blockchain participation. *Blockchain and Finance Journal, 10*(2), 177–193.

Kilsah Consulting. (2023). Empowering Women Entrepreneurs: Growth Strategies for Success. Retrieved from https://kilsahconsulting.com/women-entrepreneurs-success.

KPMG. (2022). ESG metrics that matter. Retrieved from https://kpmg.com/kpmg-us/content/dam/kpmg/pdf/2023/esg-metrics-that-matter-web-final.pdf.

McKinsey & Company. (2020a). Women as the next wave of growth in US wealth management. Retrieved from https://www.mckinsey.com/industries/financial-services/our-insights/women-as-the-next-wave-of-growth-in-us-wealth-management.

McKinsey & Company. (2020b). Women in the workplace 2020. Retrieved from https://www.mckinsey.com/featured-insights/diversity-and-inclusion/women-in-the-workplace.

McKinsey & Company. (2021a). Accounting for values and valuation. Retrieved from https://www.mckinsey.com/capabilities/strategy-and-corporate-finance/our-insights/accounting-for-values-and-valuation.

McKinsey & Company. (2021b). The rise of ESG investing: Opportunities for wealth managers. Retrieved from https://www.mckinsey.com.

McKinsey & Company. (2022a). How financial services can engage millennials and Gen Z. Retrieved from https://www.mckinsey.com.

McKinsey & Company. (2022b). The personalization imperative in financial services. Retrieved from https://www.mckinsey.com.

McKinsey & Company. (2023). *Women in fintech: Addressing the gender gap in digital finance.* Retrieved from https://www.mckinsey.com.

McKinsey & Company, & LeanIn.Org. (2020). Women in the workplace 2020. Retrieved from https://womenintheworkplace.com/2020

Merrill Lynch Wealth Management. (2018). Seeing the unseen: The role gender plays in wealth management. Retrieved from https://www.ml.com/women-research.html.

Miller, J., & Johnson, H. (2023). AI in wealth management: Biases, challenges, and solutions. *Financial Technology Review, 8*(1), 89–110.

MoneyToday. (2020, 20 January). "The Great Wealth Transfer"—are we ready for the biggest wealth transfer in history? Retrieved from https://www.moneytoday.ch/news/the-great-wealth-transfer-sind-wir-bereit-fuer-den-groessten-vermoegenstransfer-der-geschichte/.

Morgan Stanley. (2019). Sustainable signals: Individual investor interest driven by impact, conviction and choice. Retrieved from https://www.morganstanley.com/pub/content/dam/msdotcom/infographics/sustainable-investing/Sustainable_Signals_Individual_Investor_White_Paper_Final.pdf.

Morgan Stanley. (2021, June 23). Morgan Stanley launches Next Level Fund in partnership with Hearst, Microsoft, and Walmart to invest in diverse start-ups. Retrieved from https://www.morganstanley.com.

Morgan Stanley. (2023, February 7). The JumpStart program kicks into high gear. Retrieved from https://www.morganstanley.com.

Morgan Stanley. (2024, 6 November). Generation Z and millennials financial priorities. Retrieved from https://www.morganstanley.com/ideas/gen-z-millennials-financial-goals.

Morgan Stanley Centre for Sustainable Finance. (2023). The rise of impact investing: individual investors driving change. Retrieved from https://www.morganstanley.com/insights/sustainable-investing-trends-2023.

MSCI. (n.d.-a). ESG metrics. Retrieved from https://www.msci.com/ESG-Metrics.

MSCI. (n.d.-b). ESG ratings and financial performance: Research overview. Retrieved from https://www.msci.com/research-and-insights/esg-ratings-financial-performance

Netcetera. (n.d.). Banking for Gen Z: What does Gen Z really expect from their bank? Retrieved from https://www.netcetera.com/de/stories/news/banking-for-gen-z.html.

Oliver Wyman. (2020). Women in financial services. Retrieved from https://www.oliverwyman.com/our-expertise/hubs/gender-diversity-in-financial-services.html.

Pew Research Centre. (2019). Demographic trends and the rise of female wealth managers in households. Retrieved from https://www.pewresearch.org.

Precisefp. (n.d.). Understanding client demographics and evolving needs: A call for transformation in the financial advisor industry. Retrieved from https://precisefp.com/blog/understanding-client-demographics-and-evolving-needs-a-call-for-transformation-in-the-financial-advisor-industry/.

PwC. (2021). Financial services for the new generation: Meeting Millennials' and Gen Z's expectations. Retrieved from https://www.pwc.com.

Ra, M. (2023). Circular economy: Perspectives and implementation strategies. Staempfli Verlag. Retrieved from https://staempflirecht.ch/circular-economy/ean-9783727277993.

Roth, L. M. (2006). *Selling women short: Gender and money on Wall Street*. Princeton University Press.

Sifted Research. (2023). European venture capital leadership analysis. Retrieved from https://sifted.eu/research/venture-capital-europe-2023.

Smith, R., Liu, F., & Turner, B. (2023). Sustainable investing through a gender lens: How AI can support women investors. *Journal of Impact Finance, 12*(2), 302–318.

Smith, C., & Turner, S. (2015). The radical transformation of diversity and inclusion: The millennial influence. Deloitte University Leadership Centre for Inclusion. Retrieved from https://www2.deloitte.com/content/dam/Deloitte/us/Documents/about-deloitte/us-inclus-millennial-influence-120215.pdf.

Standard Chartered. (2023, 28 September). The great wealth transfer: Risks, challenges and opportunities. Financial Times. Retrieved from https://www.ft.com/partnercontent/standard-chartered/the-great-wealth-transfer-risks-challenges-and-opportunities.html.

Think Advisor. (2023, January 20). CFP diversity ticks up in 2022 Retrieved from https://www.thinkadvisor.com.

UBS. (2020). Own your worth: Why women should take control of their wealth to achieve financial well-being. UBS Investor Watch. Retrieved from https://www.ubs.com/global/en/wealth-management/women.html.

Wealth Builders Network. (2024). Strategic passive income pathways for women's financial growth. Retrieved from https://wealthbuildersnetwork.com/passive-income-women-wealth/.

Wells Fargo. (2022, December 14). Wells Fargo and Operation HOPE team up to accelerate financial inclusion. Retrieved from https://www.wellsfargo.com.

World Economic Forum. (2023). Women in leadership: The business case for gender diversity. Retrieved from https://www.weforum.org/reports/women-leadership-business-case

Chapter 5
Humanizing Wealth: Understanding Clients Beyond Assets

Rosa Sangiorgio

5.1 The Meaning of Wealth: A Multi-Faceted Concept

In the financial industry context, wealth is often seen as synonymous with assets, but these two concepts, while related, are distinct in purpose and scope. Assets are numbers on a balance sheet: stocks, bonds, real estate, cash. Wealth is something bigger: it's what those assets mean in a person's life. It's an intricate web of personal goals, legacy, relationships, all things that don't fit neatly into a spreadsheet. Recognizing these layers is essential.

Managing assets for institutional investors typically focuses on the *hard numbers*: growth and protection of financial resources, driven by return optimization, capital preservation, and risk budgeting.

Managing wealth for private clients isn't just about performance charts: it involves integrating financial decisions with the client's unique life circumstances. It's about making money work for them: for their needs, their risk comfort, and long-term priorities. While maximizing returns remains essential for private clients, it means little, if disconnected from what actually matters to them.

In this paper we will explore the complex meaning of wealth, and how wealth managers can incorporate broader definitions into their practices, from *Know Your Client (KYC)* questionnaires to the investment process itself. By understanding the essential role of values and aspirations in shaping investment strategies, wealth managers can *go beyond financial metrics* and create solutions which resonate with their clients on a personal level, consistent with the objectives of the MiFID II amendment requiring advisors to capture clients' sustainability preferences.

None of this is new. The concept of wealth has long held multiple meanings, evolving across cultures, eras, and individual perspectives: including financial

R. Sangiorgio (✉)
RSg Impact Investing, Zurich, Switzerland
e-mail: rosa@rsgimpact.com

K. Wendt, M. Ra (eds.), *Sustainable Wealth Management Revisited*, Sustainable Finance, https://doi.org/10.1007/978-3-032-02530-2_5

security—assets and resources that offer comfort and stability-as well as legacy, personal relationships, individual fulfilment, purpose, and contributions to society. What matters today is to rediscover these layers and bring them back to the heart of wealth management.

5.1.1 Historical and Modern Perspectives

In ancient societies, it was all about tangible assets—land, livestock, and goods—things that signified status and influence. Aristotle, the Greek philosopher, was probably the first to see it differently. To him, wealth wasn't the goal but a tool, a means to live a good and balanced life. In his perspective, having money was most beneficial if *it enables a person to live in accordance with their values* (Aristotle 1999, trans. Irwin).

Centuries later, economist Adam Smith (1776) defined wealth in terms of productivity, describing it as the accumulation of goods and services that benefit society. His influential work *The Wealth of Nations* underscored wealth as *a collective resource that supports societal growth*, laying the foundation for classical economics.

By the Industrial Revolution, thinkers like Karl Marx (1867) and John Stuart Mill (1848) challenged this view, examining how *wealth could lead to societal inequities if concentrated in too few hands.*

Box 5.1 Background Information: Wealth, Inequality, and Global Stability

The Uneven Distribution of Wealth

Global wealth has grown exponentially over the past century, reaching approximately $530 trillion in 2021 (Boston Consulting Group, 2022). This represents a dramatic increase from around $100 trillion in the early 1980s (McKinsey & Company, 2021). Despite this extraordinary growth, the distribution of wealth remains profoundly unequal.

According to the World Inequality Report 2023 (World Inequality Lab, 2022; Credit Suisse Research Institute, 2021), the richest 10% of the global population controls 75% of all wealth, while the bottom half holds just 2%. Wealth inequality has steadily worsened since the 1980s (Piketty, 2014), with the top 1% now owning nearly half of the world's total wealth.

Historical Context: Wealth Disparities and Instability

History has repeatedly shown that extreme wealth inequality can lead to geopolitical instability:

- The French Revolution (1789–1799): Triggered in part by stark economic inequalities, where the aristocracy controlled vast wealth while peasants faced extreme poverty.

- The Russian Revolution (1917): Economic disparity and the concentration of wealth among the nobility fuelled widespread discontent, culminating in political upheaval.
- The Arab Spring (2010–2012): Rising unemployment, food insecurity, and wealth concentration in a few hands sparked protests and revolution across the Middle East (Almond, 2012).

Modern Consequences of Inequality

1. Geopolitical Instability: Studies by the United Nations Development Programme (UNDP, 2013) reveal that countries with high levels of economic inequality are more likely to experience civil unrest, protests, and political instability.
2. Terrorism and Radicalization: Research from the World Bank (2022) links poverty and wealth disparity to increased risks of terrorism, as marginalized groups are more susceptible to radicalization when they perceive a lack of opportunity or fairness.
3. Social Fragmentation: Economic disparities exacerbate tensions within societies, weakening social cohesion and leading to political polarization and reduced trust in institutions (World Economic Forum, 2020; World Economic Forum, 2024).

The Cost to Everyone

Wealth inequality is not only a moral concern but also an economic and security issue. The World Economic Forum has highlighted income inequality as a key global risk, warning that unfair wealth distribution undermines economic growth and fuels discontent that can spill across borders (World Economic Forum, 2024).

A Call to Action

Addressing wealth inequality is essential not just for moral reasons but also for fostering a stable and prosperous world. By creating systems that enable fairer wealth distribution—through progressive taxation, universal access to education and inclusive economic policies—societies can mitigate the risks of instability and foster collective progress.

Nowadays, for many, wealth is closely tied to financial assets that provide stability and security; in parallel, a more open approach is gaining traction, among individuals who consider wealth a broader reflection of personal and social values Brunel (2006).

Contemporary thought leaders, like Jennifer Wines, have significantly advanced the multi-dimensional concept of wealth. In her book Invisible Wealth (Wines, 2023), Wines emphasizes the importance of aligning wealth with personal values: "*we're wealthy when we have an abundance of what we value.*" Financial resources are only part of a broader picture that includes health, relationships, time and purpose.

This more holistic perspective is not only theory; "*Wealth is more sophisticated than only the financial side*" stated Pinar Akiskalioglu recently on the stage of Building Bridges, representing the next generation of entrepreneurs and investors.

5.1.2 Dimensions of Wealth

To better understand wealth's many angles, this paper introduces an original framework of eight dimensions aiming to capture how individuals, families, and society interact with and define prosperity. While comprehensive in scope, this framework is not prescriptive; not all dimensions will hold equal importance for everyone. For some, just one or two may resonate, while others may find meaning in exploring multiple dimensions and their interactions. The goal is to uncover what wealth truly means to each individual in their unique context (Kinder, 2014).

These dimensions are not a hierarchy: financial resources can enable freedom, health, or education, but each dimension also carries intrinsic value that cannot be reduced to money. Their real strength lies in how they reinforce one another.

For wealth managers, the point is not to address all eight dimensions equally, but to use them as a discovery lens to uncover which matter most to the client.

To provide structure without rigidity, the framework organises the eight dimensions into three categories, from deeply personal priorities to familial and societal impact, as visible in Fig. 5.1:

- Individual: focusing on personal well-being and autonomy
- Inner Circle: emphasizing family and close relationships
- Society at Large: considering broader outward-facing responsibilities

Fig. 5.1 The eight dimensions of wealth. Note: This figure was created by the author

Individual Dimensions of Wealth

These dimensions represent the personal foundation of prosperity, focusing on the resources, opportunities, and quality of life that enable individuals to thrive. They are deeply personal, often shaping how wealth is experienced and expressed in other areas of life.

1. Financial Wealth

Represents material assets, income and investments that generates returns. For many, this is the clearest form of wealth, measured through accumulated resources and financial security.

"I want to ensure my investments to deliver solid returns without taking unnecessary risks."

2. Personal Freedom

Wealth has long been associated with freedom: the ability to make life choices and maintain control over life's direction (Li-Huang, 2018). Financial resources act as a vehicle to design a life aligned with personal goals.

"I want the freedom to take a sabbatical every five years and explore different parts of the world with my family."

3. Physical & Mental Health

"The greatest wealth is health."[1] Without physical and mental well-being, financial resources lose their meaning. This dimension emphasizes access to health care and the creation of environments that sustain long-term wellness.

"We've seen the toll that unmanaged stress can take on myself, our family and business. My goal is to establish structures that prioritize mental health and prevent burnout."

4. Intellectual Growth

Wealth is also about intellectual pursuits and opportunities for continuous learning. It allows individuals to explore passions, nurture curiosity, and engage in meaningful careers.

"I want to ensure my children can pursue careers they are passionate about, even if they aren't financially lucrative."

Inner Circle Dimensions of Wealth

These dimensions focus on the bonds that tie families and close communities together, ensuring a sense of continuity across generations. They explore the role of relationships in wealth: not just in financial terms, but in the values, support systems, and shared experiences that create lasting connections.

[1] Widely attributed to poet Virgil, albeit not clearly documented.

5. Family Legacy

Legacy reflects the desire to pass down not only assets but also family values and principles. It's about ensuring continuity and upholding a family's identity over generations.

"It's important that my family business remains a symbol of integrity and innovation for future generations."

6. Social & Relational Wealth

Relationships, within the family and the community, are essential dimensions of wealth. Social wealth is built on trust, support, and the sense of belonging that come from nurturing close relationships.

"True wealth for me is having time to be present with my family and friends."

Society at Large Dimensions of Wealth

These dimensions extend beyond the individual and family, emphasizing the wealth found in contributing to society and caring for the environment. They highlight how lasting value comes from strengthening communities and preserving resources for future generations. While distinct in their focus, the social, cultural, and environmental aspects of wealth often intersect, creating a holistic vision of impact.

7. Social & Cultural Contribution

Wealth is expressed in advancing societal progress and preserving cultural heritage. This dimension emphasises participation and engagement: from nurturing community initiatives to safeguarding traditions, arts, and values that enrich communities and provide a shared sense of identity.

"Wealth is knowing that my daughters will grow up in a society where they are not discriminated against."

8. Environmental Heritage

Environmental wealth emphasizes the stewardship of natural resources and ecosystems to ensure a liveable planet for future generations. This includes efforts to mitigate climate change, conserve biodiversity, and adopt sustainable practices.

"I want to safeguard my family's ancestral lands, ensuring they remain pristine and resilient against environmental challenges for future generations."

5.2 Integrating the Meaning of Wealth into "Know Your Client" Processes

The definition of wealth is quite personal and may materially impact the construction of an adequate portfolio for each client; wealth managers need to prioritize understanding which dimensions of wealth matter most to their clients—recognizing that these will differ from person to person—before investing their assets.

5.2.1 Traditional Approach

In general, traditional wealth management primarily focuses on aligning clients' investment portfolios with their financial risk tolerance and return expectations. This process typically involves:

Assessing Risk Tolerance: Clients complete *Know Your Client (KYC)* questionnaires or interviews to gauge their comfort with investment risk, considering factors like investment horizon, income stability, and past investment experiences.

Determining Risk Capacity: Advisors evaluate the client's financial situation to understand their ability to endure potential losses without compromising financial goals (Kahneman & Tversky, 1979).

Establishing a Risk Profile: Combining risk tolerance and capacity, advisors classify clients into categories (e.g., conservative, moderate, aggressive), guiding asset allocation decisions.

Portfolio Construction: Based on the risk profile, advisors design portfolios aiming to achieve optimal returns for the accepted risk level, often benchmarking against market indices.

While this method effectively matches financial risk with investment strategies and satisfies regulatory suitability requirements (e.g., MiFID II), it often ignores clients' broader life goals and personal values. Furthermore, the recent MiFID II amendment obliging advisors to gather clients' sustainability preferences shows that even regulators now recognise the need to look beyond risk and return (European Commission, 2021).

TIP: Wealth managers need to move beyond risk profiles and market benchmarks, gathering information and structuring investments in ways that support a client's own comprehensive definition of wealth.

5.2.2 A Comprehensive Client Discovery Process

The following process outlines one example of a structured approach to gathering comprehensive client information, blending objective financial data with subjective insights into their broader wealth perspectives.

Phase 1: Exploring the Dimensions of Wealth

These eight dimensions provide a broad lens, but they are not meant to be applied as a checklist. The wealth manager's role is to discover which of them are most relevant for each client and focus the process there.

Step 1–4: Individual Dimensions

1. Understanding Financial Wealth
   - Methodology: Use a structured *Personal Wealth Questionnaire* (*PWQ*) to collect core financial data on income, expenses, assets, liabilities.
   - Sample Question: "What financial goals are most important to you in the next 5–10 years, and how would you prioritize them?"
   - Outcome: A detailed financial profile establishing the foundation for wealth management strategies.
2. Exploring Personal Freedom
   - Methodology: Within the *PWQ*, explore personal goals like retirement and lifestyle planning, liquidity needs, and risk tolerance.
   - Sample Question: "What life events or opportunities would you like to have the financial freedom to pursue without hesitation?"
   - Outcome: A strategy ensuring sufficient liquidity and flexibility to support chosen life paths.
3. Integrating Physical & Mental Health
   - Methodology: Integrate into the *PWQ* questions to capture how clients perceive well-being as part of their wealth.
   - Sample Questions: "Have past health experiences shaped how you want to allocate resources?"; "What steps can we take to ensure that managing wealth is a source of security and not stress for you and your family?"
   - Outcome: An approach that treats health as integral to wealth preservation, ensuring clients feel secure not only financially but physically and mentally.
4. Fostering Intellectual Growth
   - Methodology: Use the *PWQ* to explore the client's intellectual interest from curiosity-driven learning to innovation.
   - Sample Questions: "Would you like to learn more about the investments in your portfolio or become more actively involved in managing them?"; "Are there areas of knowledge or expertise where you'd like to play an active role, such as mentoring others or funding innovation?"
   - Outcome: A personalized strategy that incorporates opportunities for the client to deepen their understanding of investments and play a more active role in portfolio management and allocating resources to support entrepreneurs, thus creating a legacy of intellectual and professional growth.

Step 5–6: Inner Circle Dimensions

5. Enhancing Family Legacy
   - Methodology: Facilitate *Family Workshops* to define intergenerational goals, shared values, and governance structures like family councils or charters.
   - Sample Questions: "What values or traditions do you hope to pass down to future generations, and how can wealth support that vision?"; "Are there specific structures, such as trusts or foundations, that you believe would support your legacy goals?"

- Outcome: A governance and legacy framework that preserves wealth and fosters family harmony.

6. Strengthening Social & Relational Wealth

- Methodology: Explore family cohesion, alignment of goals, and community involvement.
- Sample Question: "What steps can we take to strengthen relationships within your family and your broader community?"
- Outcome: Action plans for conflict resolution and communication within the family.

Step 7–8: Society at Large Dimensions

7. Aligning Social & Cultural Contribution

- Methodology: Deploy *ESG/Social Impact Questionnaires* to identify causes and industries aligned with the client's values, such as education, cultural preservation, or social equity (Global Impact Investing Network, 2021).
- Sample Questions: "What societal or cultural causes are closest to your heart?"; "Are there specific causes or issues you feel strongly about supporting through your investments?"
- Outcome: Impact-driven investment strategies supporting social causes and cultural heritage.

8. Advancing Environmental Heritage

- Methodology: Use *ESG/Environmental Impact Questionnaires* to assess client preferences for sustainability, conservation, and climate resilience investments.
- Sample Questions: "What environmental issues are you passionate about?"; "Do you wish to include or avoid any particular industries or practices in your portfolio?"
- Outcome: Portfolios aligned with environmental stewardship and regenerative practices.

Phase 2: Understanding the Emotional and Behavioural Landscape

Exploring the dimensions of wealth captures clients' priorities and aspirations. In order to leverage those fully, it's crucial to also understand the emotional and behavioural factors that influence how they engage with their wealth.

Whether it's their reaction to market volatility, their willingness to take risks, or their comfort with delegation, these emotional and behavioural factors play a key role in how clients approach each dimension of wealth and ultimately in financial decision making (Kahneman, 2011; Thaler, 2016). Without exploring them, even the most carefully crafted strategies can tick the box of regulatory requirements, but fall short of aligning with the client's true preferences and needs, and therefore of fulfilling fiduciary duty.

1. Identify Behavioural Patterns
   - Key Objective: Understand how the client makes decisions: are they methodical, impulsive, or reliant on external advice?
   - Methodology: Use tools, or ask open questions to evaluate decision-making styles, biases (e.g., overconfidence, loss aversion).
   - Sample Question: "Do you prefer to actively manage your wealth or rely on trusted advisors?"
   - Example of Outcome: A collaborative decision-maker may need family governance structures that engage multiple stakeholders for Family Legacy.
2. Assess Emotional Triggers
   - Key Objective: Recognize what causes stress or comfort in financial matters, such as market downturns or illiquid investments.
   - Methodology: Engage in conversations to evaluate emotional responses to financial scenarios.
   - Sample Question: "How do you typically feel when markets are volatile?"; "Do you prefer to take action or wait it out?"; "What financial decisions have caused you the most stress in the past, and why?"
   - Example of Outcome: A client prone to stress may require additional liquidity and stability when looking at Financial Strategies. Someone with a high tolerance for risk might be more open to bold investments in riskier asset classes.

This phase is critical to ensure that the insights from the dimensions of wealth are applied effectively and aligned with the client's psychological comfort.

Phase 3: Consolidating Insights into a Holistic Wealth Profile

The third phase involves integrating all the gathered information into a cohesive client profile. The most effective way to *connect the dots* is to build a dashboard to centralize and visualize client information, making it accessible for ongoing decision-making.

The idea is to build a client-centred wealth profile that serves as a living document, updated regularly to reflect changes in circumstances and priorities as visualized in Fig. 5.2.

This discovery process, while more resource-intensive, allows wealth managers to capture the full meaning of wealth for their clients and:

1. Develop personalized investment strategies that reflect what matters most to clients,
2. Foster stronger, trust-based relationships through deeper understanding and communication,

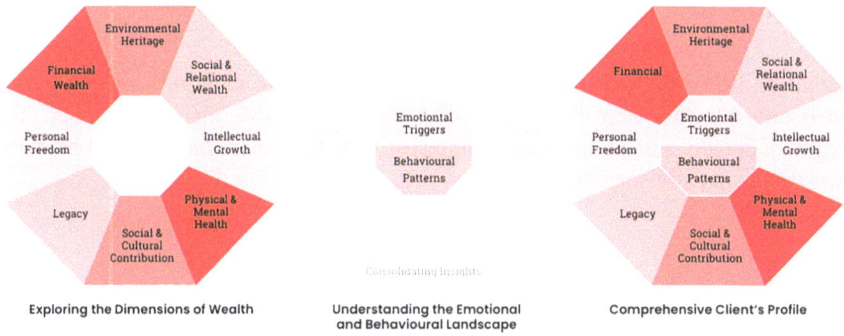

Fig. 5.2 How to build a comprehensive client's profile start. Note: This figure was created by the author

3. Enable multi-generational wealth planning, preserving not only financial assets but also family harmony and shared purpose.

Wealth managers who implement such a process position themselves as trusted partners.

TIP: Actively listen and reflect on what the client shares: ask follow-up questions to uncover deeper motivations and concerns; keep an eye on emerging technologies in areas like preference mapping and personalisation, as they will increasingly support in capturing and updating client priorities; revisit profiles regularly to ensure strategies stay aligned with evolving priorities.

Box 5.2 Jennifer Wines' Principles in Wealth Management

Jennifer Wines' *Invisible Wealth: 5 Principles for Redefining Personal Wealth in the New Paradigm* introduces five actionable principles that guide wealth managers in aligning financial strategies with clients' broader aspirations.

1. Money and Investments: What's the most important thing money buys you? What do you use money for?
2. Health & Quality of Life: At your healthiest, what else was going well for you? When do you feel the most alive?
3. Knowledge, Status & Influence: What do you want to accomplish in life? What do you want your legacy to be?
4. Time, Energy & Experiences: How do you spend most of your time? What experience made the biggest impact on your life?
5. Relationship with Self & Others: What role do the most important people play in your life? And you in theirs?

5.3 How to Use the Additional Wealth Dimensions

Gathering insights across the wealth dimensions that are most relevant to the client is only the first step: their true value lies in how those insights are used. For wealth managers, the additional challenge is to integrate these insights into practical investment and advisory processes.

5.3.1 Existing Methodologies

Few approaches are emerging that integrate wealth beyond financial returns. While still niche, they signal a shift toward multidimensional wealth management:

- Goal-Based Wealth Management: Focuses on aligning investments with specific client objectives, such as preserving generational wealth (Brunel, 2015). Each goal is assigned a dedicated sub-portfolio tailored to its timeline, risk level, and purpose. *Example:* A client might allocate a conservative portfolio to fund immediate family needs while using a growth-oriented portfolio for long-term charitable goals.
- Values-Based Investing: Aligns portfolios with an investor's ethical or societal priorities, implemented through exclusions, thematic strategies or structured approaches that adopt impact measurement frameworks like the Impact Measurement and Management ("IMM") by the Global Impact Investing Network (GIIN, 2020).
  Example: A family office prioritizes investments in renewable energy while divesting from industries with negative social impacts.
- Behavioural Finance Integration: Recognizes the influence of emotions on financial decisions, tailoring strategies to clients' psychological comfort.
  Example: A more conservative allocation is used for a client prone to anxiety during market volatility.
- Life-Centred Financial Planning: Connects wealth with life satisfaction and purpose, ensuring strategies reflect personal and family priorities.
  Example: A client reallocates resources to fund a long-held entrepreneurial dream reconnecting him/her with shared grandparents' experiences.

5.3.2 *The Opportunity of a Comprehensive Approach*

While these approaches offer useful entry points, they remain partial. The opportunity now lies in moving toward a comprehensive approach to wealth management which involves:

1. Leveraging What Exists: Build on current methodologies as starting points.
2. Incorporating Missing Dimensions: Complement these approaches to address overlooked dimensions, such as *Cultural Contribution* or *Personal Freedom.*
3. Evolve Toward Comprehensive Solutions: By building on these partial implementations, wealth managers can align their processes with a fuller understanding of wealth, ensuring that what matters most to each client — financial, emotional, relational, and/or societal — is integrated into their journey.

This evolution requires both innovation and collaboration across the wealth management industry, demonstrating that the holistic perspective of wealth is not just theoretical but a practical and impactful reality.

TIP: Prioritize relevance over exhaustiveness. Not every dimension matters equally to every client: focus on what resonates most. One size does not fit all.

Box 5.3 How Wealth Dimensions May Influence Investment Decisions
Effectively leveraging wealth's multiple dimensions includes integrating these insights into every stage of the wealth management process, ensuring alignment with long-term goals and family cohesion. You can find practical examples in the following Table 5.1.

Table 5.1 Wealth dimensions and investment decisions

Dimensions		Which role does this dimension play in investment decisions?	How can these insights be implemented?	Which governance needs to be considered?	How to measure outcomes?
Individual	**Financial wealth**	• Identifies financial return targets and appropriate level of financial security needed • Guides asset allocation, portfolio construction to align with financial goals	• Design bespoke investment portfolios • Regularly review financial strategies with governance inputs	• Implement investment committees • Clear decision-making protocols • Regular performance reviews	• Achievement of financial return targets • Adherence ex-post to agreed risk profiles
	Personal freedom	• Informs asset allocation and liquidity management, as client may need to maintain enough portfolio liquidity	• Create a liquidity reserve • Allocating part of portfolio to short-term instruments • Align fixed income portfolio with potential client's timeline • Limit portion of portfolio allocated to illiquid instruments	• Establish frameworks balancing personal autonomy and family financial goals • Periodically review	• Ability to access funds within a defined timeframe
	Physical and mental health	• Informs asset allocation, as client may need to adapt overall risk profile depending on level of stress • Informs security selections, as client may invest in health care as a theme	• Ensure ability to slight adapt risk profile if needed • Allocate a portion of investments to health-related industries.	• Define health-related priorities in family charters, constitutions and guidelines • Include health related metrics in portfolio reporting	• Improved family health metrics • Portfolios' material health related metrics improvements (e.g access to healthcare)
	Intellectual growth	• Informs asset allocation and securities selection, as client may want to: • Adapt risk profile to include stimulating asset classes (eg investments in venture capital) • Be more involved in securities' selection	• Set up educational savings accounts • Invest in entrepreneurial ventures within the family	• Establish mentorship programs or educational funding protocols in family strategies	• Number of funded entrepreneurial initiatives • Increased educational attainment within the family
Inner circle	**Family legacy**	• Informs asset allocation, as influences the time horizon of the portfolio	• Facilitate family meetings for legacy discussions • Establish trusts or endowments • Align portfolio to appropriate time horizon	• Establish family councils, constitutions, or governance boards to define legacy priorities	• Increased family engagement in legacy planning • Measurable intergenerational wealth transfer success
	Social and relational wealth	• Informs securities selection, as may drive geographical distribution (local bias)	• Organise/suggest portfolio annual family gatherings • Provide local investment opportunities	• Incorporate relationship-building into governance through regular meetings and conflict resolution	• Enhanced family relationships as reflected in participation and reduced conflicts
Society at large	**Social and cultural contribution**	• Informs asset allocation, as client may want to prioritise additional asset classes • Informs securities selection, to avoid investments with negative social impact and include those with positive social impact • Informs active ownership activities	• Screen listed investments based on identified material social metrics • Invest in sustainability linked-bonds, thematic • If risk profile permits, allocate part of portfolio to social impact investing • Engage/vote in alignment with stewardship guidelines	• Integrate social metrics in portfolio monitoring • Implement investment selection and stewardship policies to ensure alignment with client's social perspective • Publish Annual Social Impact Report	• Tangible portfolios' material social metrics improvements (e.g. access to education, jobs created)
	Environmental heritage	• Informs Asset Allocation, as client may want to prioritise additional asset classes • Informs securities selection, to avoid investments with negative environmental impact and include those with positive environmental impact • Informs active ownership activities	• Screen listed investments based on identified material environmental metrics • Invest in sustainability linked-bonds, thematic • If risk profile permits, allocate part of portfolio to environmental impact investing (private markets) • Engage/vote in alignment with stewardship guidelines	• Integrate environmental metrics in portfolio monitoring • Implement investment selection and stewardship policies to ensure investments align with client's environmental perspective • Publish Annual Environmental Impact Report	• Tangible portfolios' material environmental metrics improvements (e.g. carbon footprint, forest area restored)

Note: this table was created by the author.

Box 5.4 Case Study: Holistic Understanding of Wealth, Tribe Impact Capital

Tribe Impact Capital, a UK-based wealth management firm, offers a compelling example of how to operationalize a holistic understanding of wealth. Their proprietary ImpactDNA™ methodology demonstrates how wealth managers can integrate financial strategies with clients' values, societal aspirations, and long-term legacy goals (Tribe Impact Capital, n.d.-a).

<u>ImpactDNA™ Framework</u>

At the heart of Tribe's process is the ImpactDNA™ framework, designed to uncover and articulate clients' deeper motivations for their wealth. This process begins with an in-depth assessment that explores not just financial goals but also ethical values, family aspirations, and desired societal contributions. Clients are guided through a reflective process, resulting in a personalized ImpactDNA™ profile, which acts as a blueprint for aligning their wealth strategies with their broader life purpose.

<u>Integration with Investments</u>

Tribe's approach bridges the gap between values and investments by mapping clients' priorities to actionable investment themes. For example:

- Environmental and Social Goals: Investments are aligned with the UN Sustainable Development Goals (SDGs), focusing on areas such as climate action, education, and equity.
- Portfolio Customization: Tribe creates diversified, multi-asset portfolios that balance financial returns with measurable social and environmental outcomes. Clients can see how their investments actively contribute to their chosen impact themes (Tribe Impact Capital, n.d.-b).
- Transparency and Engagement: Through regular impact reports, clients are kept informed about how their portfolios are advancing both their financial and societal goals, fostering a sense of empowerment and connection to their investments.

5.4 Lessons from Real-Life Wealth Management

Managing wealth isn't just about making money: it's also about keeping it. And that's where many families get it wrong. You don't need to look far to find fortunes that have crumbled because of poor planning, bad decisions, or unresolved family conflicts.

Here are three stories—one disaster, one slow collapse, and one success—that show exactly what happens when wealth is, or isn't, handled wisely. They illustrate both effective and ineffective wealth management practices, highlighting the impact of goals-based alignment, legacy planning, and family governance (Cooper & Howe, 2021; IFC, 2011).

5.4.1 *The Gucci Family*

A Cautionary Tale of Family Conflict and Poor Governance

The Gucci family—founders of the luxury fashion house Gucci—exemplifies how a lack of family governance and alignment on values can lead to financial instability and loss of control. Guccio Gucci started his brand in 1921, and for a while, it was the name in Italian craftsmanship and luxury (Forden, 2000). However, by the late twentieth century, the brand became associated more with family infighting than with quality goods.

- What went wrong?Absence of Family Governance and Clear Leadership: The Gucci family lacked formal governance structures, such as family councils or boards, that might have facilitated clear communication and decision-making. Instead, decision-making was fragmented, with different family members pulling in different directions.
- Conflicting Values and Vision: With multiple family members holding stakes in the company, competing visions for the brand's future created tension. Some members wanted to protect Gucci's traditional craftsmanship, while others pushed for rapid expansion. Nobody could agree.
- No Unified Legacy or Successor Plan: The Gucci family had no clear succession plan, leadership became a battlefield. Maurizio Gucci, the last family member to hold a controlling interest, ultimately lost his stake after years of conflict.

By the 1990s, Gucci was no longer a family business. They lost control of what had once been their empire. It's a perfect example of how money alone doesn't hold a family together—shared vision and structure do.

Outcome and Lesson Learned: Governance Gaps Can Cost Control
By the 1990s, Gucci was no longer a family business. They lost control of what had once been their empire. It's a perfect example of how-without a shared vision, strong governance, and clear communication-family wealth and legacy are vulnerable to internal divisions. Had the family established structured governance, with an alignment on values and an understanding of each member's goals for the brand, they might have preserved both family control and unity.

5.4.2 *The Vanderbilt Family*

Wealth Dissipation Through Lack of Legacy Planning and Financial Discipline

Cornelius Vanderbilt, the family patriarch, built one of the greatest fortunes in the nineteenth century-and in U.S. history—through railroads and shipping (Vanderbilt, 1989). He ensured his family was wealthy, but not equipped to sustain that wealth. Within a few generations, it was all gone.

- What went wrong?No Focus on Legacy and Shared Values: Cornelius Vanderbilt left the bulk of his fortune to his son, William Henry Vanderbilt, but he didn't leave a strategy to protect it nor shared values. This meant that subsequent generations had little understanding of the values that had driven the family's initial success. His descendants inherited money, but not financial discipline.
- Absence of Wealth Education and Financial Governance: Unlike other wealthy families, the Vanderbilts did not implement family councils, governance structures, nor a real system for teaching younger generations how to manage their fortune. As the fortune was divided among numerous heirs, there was no unified approach to managing or preserving it, resulting in lavish spending without accountability. The Vanderbilt family's wealth was quickly depleted by the mid-twentieth century.

Outcome and Lessons Learned: Structured Wealth Provision is a Must
By the 1970s, none of the Vanderbilt descendants was considered wealthy by modern standards. A perfect example of how fast money can disappear without structure, discipline, and planning. Wealth managers—who aim to create lasting legacies—should encourage clients to establish family governance structures, and instil shared values that define the family's approach to wealth. Those structures can play a crucial role in protecting wealth from dilution over generations.

5.4.3 The Rockefeller Family

A Model of Structured Wealth Preservation and Value Alignment

John D. Rockefeller, founder of Standard Oil, was one of the wealthiest individuals in history. Unlike other wealthy families, though, he made sure his family had the tools to preserve and even grow their wealth over generations (Chernow, 1998).

- What they did right?Created a Family Office and Formal Governance**:** They established one of the first family offices in the United States, providing a structured approach to managing family assets, philanthropy, and governance. This facilitated centralized decision-making and provided professional management, helping the family navigate financial and generational transitions.
- Committed to Shared Values**:** John D. Rockefeller established a strong philanthropic tradition, and his descendants embraced it. Having a bigger purpose beyond just making money kept them united.
- Strategic Use of Trusts and Succession Planning: The Rockefellers set up financial structures which provided financial stability across generations, while reducing the risk of wealth dilution. By establishing clear succession plans and educating younger family members in financial stewardship, the Rockefellers ensured that family wealth would be managed responsibly.

Outcome and Lessons Learned: Financial Success Across Generations Depends on Governance and Legacy Planning

The Rockefeller family remains financially successful and influential nowadays, with family members continuing to engage in philanthropic and investment activities aligned with the original values of John D. Rockefeller (Rockefeller Foundation, 2022). This success is attributed to the family's commitment to governance, legacy planning, and education in financial responsibility. By prioritizing a holistic approach to wealth management that incorporates family values and strategic planning, the Rockefellers have created a sustainable legacy.

The Takeaway: Without planning, even great fortunes can vanish.

- Money itself isn't enough: a family without structure will lose its wealth, no matter how much they start with.
- Ignoring governance is a mistake: without clear leadership, conflicts will tear a family business apart.
- Teach financial discipline: if younger generations don't understand money, they won't keep it.
- Values matter: a shared purpose keeps a family united—and wealth intact.

TIP: To avoid *Wealth Erosion* support your clients to prioritize *Governance*, *Trust Structures*, and align *Family Values.*

5.5 Conclusion

Wealth is more than money, and managing it takes more than numbers.

A truly multidimensional approach to wealth management is essential, but it comes with challenges. Understanding each client's values takes time, adapting strategies to their needs requires flexibility, and executing those strategies effectively depends on having the right resources. Without these, even the best financial plans risk overlooking what truly matters to clients.

The best wealth managers will be those who never stop learning, evolving, and collaborating across disciplines. Technology, particularly data-driven personalization and emerging AI tools, will play a crucial role in this transformation, helping to uncover deeper insights, track shifting priorities, and improve decision-making. But technology alone isn't the answer. Real impact will come from those who ask better questions, listen more deeply, and create solutions that go beyond preserving wealth to ensuring it serves a meaningful purpose.

The future of wealth management belongs to those who look beyond the numbers. Those who embrace innovation, build stronger relationships, and adapt to an ever-changing world will be the ones who redefine what it means to manage wealth. Because in the end, wealth should serve people, not the other way around.

References

Almond, M. (2012). The Arab Spring: Contemporary revolutions in historical comparison. *All Azimuth, 1*(2), 35–53.

Aristotle. (1999). Nicomachean ethics (T. Irwin, Trans.). Hackett Publishing Company.

Boston Consulting Group. (2022). *Global wealth report 2022.* https://www.bcg.com/publications/2022/standing-still-not-an-option. Accessed March 2025.

Brunel, J. L. P. (2006). *Integrated wealth management: The new direction for portfolio managers.* Institutional Investor Books.

Brunel, J. L. P. (2015). *Goals-based wealth management: An integrated and practical approach to changing the structure of wealth advisory practices.* Wiley.

Chernow, R. (1998). Titan: The life of John D. Rockefeller, Sr. Random House.

Cooper, A., & Howe, K. (2021). *Vanderbilt: The rise and fall of an American Dynasty.* HarperCollins.

Credit Suisse Research Institute. (2021). *Global wealth report.* https://www.credit-suisse.com/about-us/en/reports-research/global-wealth-report.html. Accessed March 2025.

European Commission. (2021). Commission Delegated Regulation (EU) 2021/1253 amending MiFID II as regards the integration of sustainability factors and preferences. Official Journal of the European Union. https://eur-lex.europa.eu/legal-content/EN/TXT/?uri=CELEX:32021R1253

Forden, S. G. (2000). *The house of Gucci: A sensational story of murder, madness, glamour, and greed.* HarperCollins.

Global Impact Investing Network (GIIN). (2021). *Impact measurement and management in practice.* https://iris.thegiin.org/imm-in-practice/. Accessed March 2025.

Global Impact Investing Network (GIIN). (2020). *State of impact measurement and management practice.* https://thegiin.org/publication/research/imm-survey-second-edition/. Accessed March 2025.

International Finance Corporation. (2011). *Family business governance handbook.* https://www.ifc.org/en/insights-reports/2011/ifc-family-business-governance-handbook. Accessed March 2025.

Kahneman, D. (2011). Thinking, fast and slow. Farrar, Straus and Giroux.

Kahneman, D., & Tversky, A. (1979). Prospect theory: An analysis of decision under risk. *Econometrica, 47*(2), 263–292.

Kinder, G. E. (2014). Life planning for you: How to design & deliver the life of your dreams. Life Planning Media.

Li-Huang, R. (2018). The psychology of high net worth individuals. Harvard business review. In H. K. Baker, G. Filbeck, & V. Ricciardi (Eds.), *Financial behavior: Players, services, products, and markets* (pp. 173–191). Oxford University Press. https://ssrn.com/abstract=2980721. Accessed March 2025

Marx, K. (1867). *Das Kapital: Critique of political economy.* Verlag von Otto Meissner.

McKinsey & Company. (2021). *The rise and rise of the global balance sheet.* https://www.mckinsey.com/industries/financial-services/our-insights/the-rise-and-rise-of-the-global-balance-sheet-how-productively-are-we-using-our-wealth. Accessed March 2025.

Mill, J. S. (1848). *Principles of political economy.* John W. Parker.

Piketty, T. (2014). *Capital in the Twenty-First Century.* Harvard University Press.

Rockefeller Foundation. (2022). *Impact report 2020–2022.* https://www.rockefellerfoundation.org/news-and-insights/impact-reports/impact-report-2023/. Accessed March 2025.

Smith, A. (1776). *An inquiry into the nature and causes of the wealth of nations.* W. Strahan and T. Cadell.

Thaler, R. H. (2016). *Misbehaving: The making of behavioral economics*. W.W. Norton & Company.

Tribe Impact Capital. (n.d.-a). *B Corp finance coalition UK calls for legal change to finance companies' governance frameworks*. https://tribeimpactcapital.com/impact-hub/b-corp-finance-coalition-uk-calls-for-legal-change-to-finance-companies-governance-frameworks/. Accessed March 2025.

Tribe Impact Capital. (n.d.-b). *Our approach: Your ImpactDNA*. https://tribeimpactcapital.com/investing-with-us/our-approach/your-impactdna/. Accessed March 2025.

United Nations Development Programme. (2013). Humanity divided: Confronting inequality in developing countries. UNDP. https://www.undp.org/publications/humanity-divided-confronting-inequality-developing-countries. Accessed March 2025.

Vanderbilt, A. T. (1989). *Fortune's children: The fall of the house of Vanderbilt*. William Morrow & Co.

Wines, J. (2023). *Invisible wealth: 5 principles for redefining personal wealth in the new paradigm*. Wiley.

World Bank. (2022). Poverty and shared prosperity 2022. https://www.worldbank.org/en/publication/poverty-and-shared-prosperity. Accessed March 2025.

World Economic Forum. (2024). Global risks report 2024. https://www.weforum.org/publications/global-risks-report-2024/. Accessed March 2025.

World Inequality Lab. (2022). World inequality report 2022. https://wir2022.wid.world/. Accessed March 2025.

Chapter 6
Sustainable Investing, the New Normal in Wealth Management

Tina Minci and Monika Seppi

6.1 Client Preferences and Sustainable Products in the Market

6.1.1 Sustainability on the Raise

Sustainable finance has gained more focus in the financial industry, notably in wealth management as more investors want to understand the role and impact that sustainability can have on their financial decisions. This awareness has increased the emphasis on environmental, social, and governance (ESG) factors and the respective impact of investment choices, leading to considerations of these elements in investment selections (Auzepy et al., 2024).

A recent study by Morgan Stanley on global wealth highlights that interest in sustainable investing has risen. As driving factors are mentioned inflationary pressures, recent findings on climate change, and the positive financial performance of sustainable investments. The study further showed that investors who believed their sustainable investments were underperforming in 2022 remained still determined to continue the sustainable investment approach, suggesting a preference for long-term value creation despite of short-term market instability (Morgan Stanley, 2024a).

This can suggest changes in preferences, where investors with sustainability preferences prioritize long-term impact, despite of possible short-term underperformance.

T. Minci (✉) M. Seppi
Women In Sustainable Finance (WISF), Zurich, Switzerland
e-mail: tina.minci@wisfinternational.com

K. Wendt, M. Ra (eds.), *Sustainable Wealth Management Revisited*, Sustainable Finance, https://doi.org/10.1007/978-3-032-02530-2_6

6.1.2 Generational Change Will Trigger More Interest in Sustainable Finance

One of the crucial drivers behind this development is the generational change. Several studies show that younger investors are far more intrigued to explore and opt for sustainable investment options (Forbes, 2022; BCG, 2022).

This generational change is encouraging financial institutions to innovate and introduce new offerings, adapting to sustainability-minded clients and influencing how inherited wealth is managed. As in the next decades it is expected that the younger generations will inherit large amounts of wealth, they are expected to continue this trend, influencing the industry to align closely investment priorities with sustainability preferences into the core of wealth management (WEF, 2022; NASDAQ, 2022; Forbes, 2023).

6.1.3 Market Developments Still Diverge

The market has responded swiftly to these evolving preferences. Financial institutions have launched a broad range of ESG-focused products exploring different approaches to include risks and or opportunities dedicated to sustainability themes.

In terms of financial performance, there are several studies indicating underperformance as well as competitive and superior performance, making it difficult to have an overall conclusion (Amundi, 2024; Morningstar, 2024b; Financial Times, 2024; Morgan Stanley, 2024b).

Sustainable investments flows are seeing as well different developments in different regions of the world. In the USA there have been significant outflows from sustainability focused funds among others due to political and regulatory backlash. The developments in the EU and several Asian markets show instead support for sustainability focused funds, with Asian markets supported by government-sponsored green finance initiatives, while European markets continue to attract inflows due to consistent regulatory developments (Morgan Stanley, 2024c Morningstar, 2024a; UNTACT, 2024; SSF, 2024).

It is expected that sustainability will stay in the financial industry, driven by the global regulatory landscape and with divergent development across regions.

6.2 Regulatory Landscape Fostering Sustainable Finance Investments in Wealth Management

6.2.1 The Regulatory Wave

The EU's Action Plan for Sustainable Finance is one of the most ambitious initiatives globally. It emphasized the need for clear transparency in the financial markets on how sustainability is being incorporated in financial products (European Commission, 2018). The EU Sustainable Finance Disclosure Regulation "SFDR" is a disclosure framework for financial products, which should help investors to better understand the sustainability risks and impacts of a product (European Union, 2019). In order to support the transition to a green economy, the EU further defined a classification system and standardized definitions of what qualifies as environmentally sustainable economic activities under the EU Taxonomy (European Union, 2020). The regulation is expected to expand and to cover more economic activities as well.

Despite of the introduced regime, which requires disclosures of substantial sustainability information in the fund disclosures, there have been increased concerns of greenwashing, as many funds have been marketed as sustainable or ESG-focused, without a transparent sustainability characteristic (EBA, 2024).

The European Securities and Markets Authority (ESMA) has therefore established clear criteria and standards for fund labels to make sure that these labels correctly reflect the fund's sustainability profile (ESMA, 2024). The guidance aims to equip investors with clear and consistent information, while reducing the risk of misleading labelling, and improve the comparability across funds.

In Switzerland, the practice has been led by a softer, more principle-based environment. The Swiss Federal Council has issued its position on preventing greenwashing in the financial sector and emphasized the importance of transparency and clear standards. The position paper further introduced the definition of sustainable investments for the Swiss market (Swiss Federal Council, 2022).

The Swiss Financial Market Authority (FINMA) further emphasized in its supervisory notice expectations for transparency in sustainability-related disclosures for collective investment schemes, stressing the need of accurate and clear information in marketing and product documentation (FINMA, 2021). The different initiatives have been further complemented by new self-regulatory guidelines from the Swiss Bankers Association (SBA, 2024), which have been updated in 2024.

Other wealth management hubs have introduced similar frameworks, such as the UK with the Sustainable Disclosure Regulation (SDR), which include different rules on anti-greenwashing, naming and labelling and product level disclosures (FCA, 2023) The UK also started the consultation on a UK Green Taxonomy following the Green Technical Advisory Group (GTAG)'s work on the UK Green Taxonomy for financial and non-financial firms (HM Treasury, 2024).

Singapore, as another major hub for wealth management, has as well introduced similar initiatives. The Singapore's Monetary Authority of Singapore (MAS) has introduced the Taxonomy for Sustainable Finance as well as reporting requirements for ESG retail funds (MAS, 2022, 2023).

In the USA, the developments have been less intense, when it comes to the scope of the regulatory work. The Securities and Exchange Commission (SEC) has introduced for instance amendments to the Investment Company Act "Names Rule" and requires fund managers to disclose for the funds, whose names suggest a focus in a particular type of investment to adopt a policy to invest at least 80 percent of the value of their assets in those investments. Therefore, fund managers are required to disclose the criteria when labelling funds with ESG terms (SEC, 2023).

However, there aren't defined standards in the USA for measuring sustainability impact, for example through a taxonomy.

Generally, the developments are going in similar directions, while the EU has been a leading example for other wealth management hubs, which are implementing similar initiatives, contributing to a global push for sustainability in finance in the wealth management practice.

6.2.2 Collecting Client Sustainability Preferences

The requirement to collect sustainable finance preferences for private clients varies across countries and has not established broadly in many jurisdictions. The sustainability preferences collection is currently regulated in the EU under MiFID II for investment firms offering advice or portfolio management (European Union, 2021). In Switzerland the collection of sustainability preferences is treated under the SBA's self-regulation and therefore, mandatory for members of the SBA. Although the sustainability preferences collection of clients has not been formalized in the UK as in the EU or Switzerland for some financial institutions, the British Financial Conduct Authority (FCA)'s Sustainability Disclosure Rules (SDR) emphasizes the requirements for distributors to ensure that product-level information (including the labels) is made available to consumers. The marketing material should support consumers with clearer information to better understand the key sustainability features of a product (FCA, 2023).

The intention of these regulations and guidance is to encourage conversations between clients and advisors about sustainability and raising awareness around ESG risks and opportunities. The dialogue should as well support knowledge building to help clients understand the implications of ESG characteristics in their investments.

Other countries are not yet approaching the topic or do so rather implicitly. Some of the recommendations encourage financial institutions to integrate ESG considerations into their advisory or product offerings, but no explicit preference collection is required as for example in Australia (ASFI, 2020).

6.2.3 Effectiveness of Current Regimes

Looking at the European regime for collecting sustainability preferences, the definition of sustainable preferences under EU MiFID II limits the scope of sustainable investing possibilities to the ones defined under the EU SFDR and EU Taxonomy Regulation. The system in its current shape is complex to advise and as well from a client perspective too difficult to understand (FNG, 2022; AIPB, 2022). Firms can still recommend products that do not meet the sustainability preferences of the client, but only if the client adapts (relaxes) its preferences, which can be in practice very burdensome.

A key criticism is that selecting a "sustainable" profile under MiFID II restricts clients only to investments deemed sustainable by very narrow criteria. Once a client indicates a preference for sustainable investments, the scope of potential investment options reduces, as the products that can be selected have to be aligned with the clients' sustainability profile. This lack of flexibility combined with the complexity of the framework can prevent clients from selecting a sustainable category.

The study by Kölbel and Weder (2024) found that while fewer clients are formally categorized as "sustainable," they often still hold a certain number of sustainable products in their portfolios. This suggests that simply categorizing clients based on sustainability preferences may not necessarily lead to an increase in sustainable investment allocations, and future revisions to MiFID II may be necessary.

Switzerland's SBA guidelines on sustainable preferences in comparison is less complex in terms of frameworks used and provide more flexibility by permitting clients with sustainable preferences to also invest in non-sustainable products where financial interests are higher weighted (SBA, 2024). This flexibility incentivizes a more practical approach to sustainability, enabling wealth managers to offer diverse options and clients to focus on sustainable investments without overly restricting the investment universe, potentially limiting diversification, risk management and other performance of their investment portfolios.

6.2.4 Outlook

As sustainable finance evolves, these diverse regulatory approaches highlight the need for adaptable frameworks that support both sustainable growth and agility and financial resilience, while addressing clients' increasing interest in sustainability in a way which is easily understandable for them.

This process is a learning journey, while the basis for this journey is to properly understand what sustainability is, and how the different sustainable finance strategies work in wealth management.

6.3 Understanding ESG Strategies

6.3.1 *What Is ESG Investing?*

It is an investment approach, where ESG factors are taken into consideration in the investment decision process alongside traditional financial analysis. At this point, there is no universal definition of ESG investing, but this approach aims to manage risks and capitalize on opportunities (see Table 6.1) by considering issues like climate change, natural resource use, human capital practices, community relations and corporate governance standards (OECD, 2020).

6.3.2 *The Evolution of ESG Investing*

The concept traces back to the eighteenth century when environmental factors began shaping economic decisions. Early examples of values-based investing include the establishment of the US Pioneer Fund in 1928, which avoided sectors like alcohol and tobacco (Renneboog et al., 2007). In the 1980s, divestment campaigns against South Africa's apartheid regime brought more attention to ethical investing. Sustainability gained global recognition in 1987 with the Brundtland Commission's report Our Common Future, defining sustainable development as "meeting the needs of the present without compromising the ability of future generations to meet their own needs." This linked environmental concerns with social and economic issues, laying the foundation for frameworks like John Elkington's Triple Bottom Line (1997), which emphasized the interconnectedness of environmental, social, and financial performance.

The term ESG appeared in the 2004 United Nations report Who Cares Wins, which provided guidelines for integrating ESG factors into financial services. This, alongside the UN's Freshfields Report, highlighted ESG's financial relevance, leading to the 2006 launch of the Principles for Responsible Investment (PRI). This was a significant milestone for integrating ESG considerations in mainstream finance and investment decisions (Eccles et al., 2020).

Table 6.1 Summary of ESG factors (Own illustrations, 2024)

Environmental factors	Social factors	Governance factors
• Managing climate impact by reducing pollution, controlling emissions, and addressing climate risks • Ensuring efficient use of resources, like energy, water, and raw materials while limiting the adverse impact on nature and in particular biodiversity	• Management of human resources, community relations, and animal welfare • Sustainable relationships between society, environment, and community well-being	• Efficient decision-making processes and structures within organizations • Compliance and alignment with regulation, industry standards, and stakeholder interests

ESG investing has recently shifted from institutional only focus to private wealth management. The anticipated wealth transfer from baby boomers to their heirs over the next two decades highlights the growing influence of next-generation investors who prioritize sustainability (Cerulli Associates, 2022). Integrating ESG into wealth management enables the wealth transfer process to align with personal and family values, ensuring a values-driven approach to intergenerational planning (EY, 2023). Through sustainable trusts, ESG focused family foundations, and aligned investments and philanthropy, wealth can contribute to social and environmental goals, preserving family values and creating lasting impact. Furthermore, it also provides a robust framework for portfolio resilience, protecting financial performance and family legacies from risks (IMD, 2024) such as climate change, regulatory shifts, and disruptive trends.

6.3.3 ESG Investment Strategies in Wealth Management

Wealth management employs tailored ESG approaches to reflect family and personal values. Figure 6.1 illustrates the most widely utilized strategies.

Now, let us examine each strategy in greater detail:

Screening, in particular exclusionary screening is a popular strategy, allowing high-net-worth individuals to exclude industries like fossil fuels or firearms that conflict with their principles. Positive screening and best-in-class approaches offer another route, selecting sustainability leaders across sectors.

ESG integration represents a sophisticated method of systematically embedding environmental, social, and governance (ESG) factors into conventional financial analysis. By assessing material ESG risks and opportunities, investors can develop a more holistic understanding of a company's long-term potential. This

Fig. 6.1 ESG investment strategies in wealth management (Own illustrations, 2024)

strategy has become widely utilized in both active and passive investment management to strengthen portfolio resilience (SSF, 2017).

Thematic investing further support alignment with family or individual missions. Thematic investing targets specific ESG themes, such as renewable energy, water conservation, or gender equality. This approach enables investors to allocate capital to sectors that promote positive environmental or social outcomes, often aiming to foster long-term structural changes within society (SSF, 2017).

Impact investing can be employed by wealthy individuals with the aim to generate measurable social or environmental benefits alongside financial returns (Bugg-Levine & Emerson, 2011). Unlike ESG investing, which focuses on mitigating risks and improving returns, impact investing prioritizes achieving specific, quantifiable outcomes while maintaining financial sustainability. According to the Global Impact Investing Network (GIIN), its core principles include intentionality, measurable impact, and a financial return expectation, ranging from below-market to market rate (GIIN, 2023).

Active ownership provides asset owners with a unique opportunity to engage directly with companies and exercise voting rights, ensuring their investments align with long-term objectives (Dimson et al., 2015). This approach often proves more effective than divestments in case of value misalignment and perfectly complements the other strategies, as direct engagement can drive meaningful change within companies. Given its growing significance over the past decade, this strategy will be explored in greater detail in Sect. 6.5.

These various ESG investment approaches offer a diverse range of strategies, from simple exclusions to proactive engagement and targeted impact. Each approach provides a unique way to balance financial returns with environmental, social, and governance considerations. Importantly, these different approaches are not mutually exclusive but can be combined to suit specific investment goals, leading to numerous nuances and tailored solutions. Overall, ESG strategies in wealth management can align financial security with ethical principles and tailor to each individual's or family's unique goals.

6.4 Overview of SGDs

6.4.1 What Are the Sustainable Development Goals?

The Sustainable Development Goals (SDGs) emerged from the need for a comprehensive approach to development—one that integrates economic growth, social well-being, and environmental health (United Nations, 2015). They evolved from the Millennium Development Goals (MDGs), which were established by the United Nations in 2000 to tackle poverty, hunger, and other pressing issues in developing nations. By 2012, it was evident that the MDGs fell short of addressing the broader and more complex global challenges. At the Rio + 20 Conference in 2012, representatives from member states, NGOs, and civil society recognized the need for a more universal framework to guide all nations toward a sustainable future. Following extensive consultations, the United Nations launched the Sustainable Development Goals in 2015 as part of the 2030 Agenda for Sustainable Development. These 17 goals, supported by 169 specific targets, address interconnected global challenges such as ensuring quality education, providing access to clean water and sanitation, combating climate change, reducing inequality, and promoting sustainable development across economic, social, and environmental dimensions. Unlike the MDGs, the SDGs require contributions from all countries—regardless of development status—emphasizing that sustainability must encompass economic, social, and environmental dimensions for a balanced, resilient future. Moreover, the SDGs call for collaboration across all sectors—governments, corporations, NGOs, and individuals—to collectively pursue a sustainable world by 2030.

6.4.2 SDGs Aligned Investing

ESG investing integrates ESG factors into financial decision-making to manage risks and identify growth opportunities, thereby enhancing long-term, risk-adjusted returns (OECD, 2020). SDGs investing goes beyond that and aims to actively generate positive social and environmental outcomes that directly align with the SDGs (Global Investors for Sustainable Development [GISD] Alliance, 2020). While ESG offers a broad sustainability framework, SDGs aligned investing focuses on specific, measurable contributions toward the 17 SDGs, creating direct, quantifiable impacts, such as increasing access to clean water (SDG 6) or affordable and clean energy (SDG 7).

Within the wealth management context, SDGs investing can play a vital role in helping high-net-worth individuals and families connect their wealth with broader societal goals (Päetzold et al., 2022). The framework provides a purposeful, goal-oriented approach to investing, offering an opportunity to shape their legacy by directing wealth towards specific outcomes, such as ensuring access to clean water (SDG 6) or promoting quality education (SDG 4).

The ESG investment approaches outlined in the previous section can be adapted to align more specifically with the SDGs. Each approach, from exclusionary screening to impact investing, can be fine-tuned to ensure that investments not only mitigate risks and identify opportunities but also directly or indirectly contribute to achieving global sustainability targets.

Screening, in particular exclusionary screening remains a popular strategy for SDGs investing, allowing high-net-worth individuals to exclude industries in conflict with specific SDGs. For instance, exclusionary screening can be used to avoid investments in industries that undermine SDGs, such as coal.

ESG integration involves systematically incorporating SDGs factors into traditional financial analysis. For instance, a company that actively works on reducing emissions would be evaluated not only based on its financial health but also on its contribution to climate action (SDG 13). The integration approach ensures that SDGs metrics are part of the fundamental financial evaluation of the company.

Thematic investing can be particularly impactful when targeting SDGs—such as focusing on clean water initiatives (SDG 6) or gender equality (SDG 5)—creating a positive impact aligned with specific, measurable outcomes.

Impact investing targets measurable contributions to SDGs alongside financial returns, going beyond traditional ESG integration. For family offices or wealthy individuals, it offers a values-driven strategy, enabling investments in areas like renewable energy (SDG 7) that align with family legacy goals while delivering both financial and societal or environmental impact.

Active ownership enhances SDGs focused wealth management by allowing asset owners to directly influence corporate practices toward social and environmental goals rather than simply divest in case of value misalignment. Through targeted engagement, wealthy individuals can push for SDGs aligned changes, such as encouraging companies to set diversity targets for gender equality (SDG 5). As mentioned in the previous section, given its growing significance over the past decade, this strategy will be explored in greater detail in Sect. 6.5.

6.4.3 Funding Solutions for SDGs

While the investment gap to achieve the SDGs remains substantial, estimated between $2.5 and $4.0 trillion annually in developing countries (United Nations Inter-agency Task Force on Financing for Development, 2024), there is significant potential for wealth management to bridge this gap. Areas like affordable and clean energy (SDG 7), clean water and sanitation (SDG 6), and industry innovation and infrastructure (SDG 9) are in particular need of funding.

To address these gaps, SDGs investing may direct capital through thematic funds focused on sectors like renewable energy, healthcare, and clean water. Green and social bonds target projects with environmental or social benefits—green bonds can finance renewable energy, while social bonds may support affordable housing and healthcare. Development impact bonds and sustainability-linked loans also promote sustainability by aligning financial returns with specific SDGs. Private equity and venture capital play a key role in advancing SDG-aligned businesses by providing long-term capital and supporting startups, such as those driving innovations in climate technology and financial inclusion. Similarly, debt financing from development banks or private institutions helps fund socially impactful initiatives. Public-private partnerships, especially through blended finance models, can reduce risks and incentivize private sector investment in projects that would otherwise lack funding (OECD, 2018).

In summary, ESG investing builds resilience by integrating ESG factors to manage risks and capitalize on opportunities. SDGs investing, however, targets specific measurable contributions to UN-defined goals. By integrating SDGs principles into wealth management, families can combine financial returns with concrete social and environmental contributions, ultimately ensuring their legacy has a positive and measurable impact on the world.

6.5 Stewardship (Active Ownership) in Wealth Management

Stewardship (or active ownership) has been a key instrument for institutional investors and is becoming increasingly important in wealth management (CSP, 2022).

Stewardship is a strategy that allows investors to influence the companies they invest in. Stewardship activities include the identification, monitoring, and integration in investment and stewardship decisions of material sustainability-related risks and opportunities that impact long-term value creation (ICGN, 2024).

This approach enables clients, through their wealth manager, to take part in key corporate decisions, often by delegating their voting rights. In this setup, the wealth manager is responsible for exercising these rights in the client's best interest, adhering therefore, to fiduciary duty (UNPRI, 2022, 2021).

The United Nations Principles for Responsible Investments (UNPRI, 2024a) defines stewardship as:

> Stewardship is the use of investor rights and influence to protect and enhance overall long-term value for clients and beneficiaries, including the common economic, social and environmental assets on which their interests depend.

6.5.1 Proxy Voting

Proxy voting is one of the most common tools of stewardship, giving investors the possibility to make decisions on corporate matters without needing to attend annual meetings in person. Proxy voting gives shareholders the possibility to delegate their voting power to a representative, to vote on their behalf on different matters, including sustainability-matters (Hirst, 2016).

Wealth managers generally rely on proxy advisory firms or depending on the size of the organization and priorities on inhouse sustainability knowhow to guide voting recommendations, making sure that votes align with the long-term interests (FRC, 2020).

6.5.2 Engagement

In addition to proxy voting, direct engagement with companies is a crucial mechanism. Engagement is conducted through meetings or other means of exchange with corporate boards and executives, like for example official letters (UNPRI, 2018).

For wealth management clients, engagement represents another form of influence beyond proxy voting. Through dialog, wealth managers can flag issues related to sustainability matters and can request to adopt practices that align with their clients' values.

6.5.3 *Individual or Collective Engagement*

Individual engagement focuses on direct, one-to-one dialogue that focuses on concerns related to sustainability-matters, while collective engagement addresses as the terminology suggests combined engagement activities and resources of several investors with the aim to drive a larger change and address sustainability issues more efficiently (UNPRI, 2024b).

Collective engagement is usually driven by specialized organizations that focus on particular topics as the Climate 100+[1] or that have a broader approach to sustainability matters as the UNPRI.

Individual engagement allows wealth managers to directly align the engagement goals with internal sustainability strategies, policies and client preferences, allowing a proactive approach to address relevant topics and tailor therefore, any engagement efforts (UNPRI, 2021).

However, it can be resource-intensive, as direct engagement requires significant time, effort and knowhow, which can be limited depending on the topic of engagement.

Collective engagement on the other hand can have greater and faster impact, as the investee company faces more pressure when several investors collectively voice a sustainability concern. This sets increased risk of greater investment withdrawals or share selloffs if the investor requests are not taken seriously. On the other side, cost efficiency is another advantage by sharing efforts. On the downside, coordinating diverse investor priorities can be difficult and time-intense, and there is a risk of not aligning the engagement efforts with specific strategies of investors (UNPRI, 2018).

For wealth managers, the decision between individual and collective engagement should be based on clients' priorities and internal resources, balancing individual engagement goals with the broader impact and cost-efficiency of collective strategies.

[1] Climate 100+ is an organization which focuses among else on the climate Engagement. See under https://www.climateaction100.org/.

6.5.4 Voluntary Stewardship Codes

There are multiple frameworks available to support financial institutions in establishing effective active ownership practice. International guidelines such as the one from the UNPRI and ICGN provide standards for engagement, proxy voting, and ESG integration. Several countries have developed stewardship codes to promote responsible investment and sustainable value creation through active engagement with focus on institutional investors.

Most of the stewardship codes are modelled after the UK Stewardship Code 2010/2012, while all use generally non-binding wording (Katelouzu & Puchniak, 2021). Core differences are seen on terminologies.

The focus has undergone some changes: in the beginning more attention was given to governance topics. New stewardship codes or updates to existing ones (e.g. updated UK Stewardship Code 2020) include newly environmental and social matters and go beyond corporate governance. This concept reflects a more holistic approach to stewardship. Some newly developed stewardship codes specifically focus on sustainability value creation (e.g. Swiss Active Ownership Code by AMAS and SSF).

International frameworks for net zero transition plans (e.g. Glasgow Financial Alliance for Net Zero "GFANZ) are setting a particular emphasis on stewardship, requiring to disclosure how engagement is being incorporated in organizations, highlighting that collaboration and influence are more effective for triggering change than divestments, particularly for high-emitting sectors (IPSF, 2024).

6.5.5 Frameworks and Regulations Incorporating Stewardship

Several regulatory frameworks have been evolving and have implemented elements related to stewardship.

The European Union's Shareholder Rights Directive II (SRD II), for example, requires financial institutions which are in scope of the directive to disclose their policies for engaging with companies, which should include how they monitor and can influence investee companies (European Union, 2017). This directive aims to enhance transparency, making it easier for clients to understand how their wealth managers are representing their interests. Other regulations as "SFDR" require disclosures as well around engagement policies that the financial market participants have implemented in their organizations (European Union, 2019).

In the U.S., the Securities and Exchange Commission (SEC) has increased scrutiny around proxy voting practices, emphasizing the need for investment managers to act in the best interests of clients when making voting decisions (SEC, 2019).

This means that investment managers are increasingly accountable for aligning their active ownership strategies with clients' expectations, whether those are centered on financial returns or ethical concerns.

6.5.6 Outlook for Stewardship

As clients prioritize sustainability considerations, stewardship is expected to play a more central role in wealth management. In this future landscape, stewardship will not only be about exercising voting rights at shareholder meetings but also about fostering an ongoing dialogue with clients and streamlining meaningful actions towards key sustainability matters as climate. This shift would lead to a more personalized wealth management, where clients are actively involved in shaping their investments and achieving impact beyond financial returns. This will mean as well that more knowledge building and sharing will be required for wealth management professionals and clients.

6.6 Case Studies in ESG in Wealth Management

For this case study in ESG aligned wealth management, consider a family business focused on real estate, where the older generation is preparing for wealth transfer, and younger members are increasingly involved in decision-making.

The older generation is particularly interested in leaving a legacy that gives back to the community and has chosen to invest part of its business in green-certified real estate projects that emphasize affordable housing. Additionally, it seeks philanthropic advice to develop community-focused initiatives that align with the family's values. The younger members, who are poised to inherit both the portfolio and the family business, express a growing interest in a more sustainable investment approach besides the philanthropic activities already in place by the older generation, particularly with a thematic focus on social equality. They wish to reallocate part of the traditional assets into sustainable investments that directly impact social outcomes. Additionally, they plan to spin off part of the family business to focus on innovative real estate solutions that can help reduce carbon emissions in an industry that has been difficult to decarbonize. This reflects the younger generations' proactive stance toward addressing climate change while modernizing the business.

The wealth manager's role is to facilitate this transition by aligning the family's wealth management strategies with evolving values across generations. This typically includes offering investment advice that incorporates ESG principles. In this specific case, it may be suitable to offer a core-satellite approach (to ensure diversification), where part of the portfolio is invested in impact funds focusing on social equality as requested by the younger generation. However, this example demonstrates how ESG in wealth management is not limited to portfolio construction, but also involves guiding the family through estate planning, philanthropic advice and providing education and expertise access. Concretely, this can be achieved by connecting the younger generation with experts on the decarbonization of the real estate sector to support the business spin-off or by introducing the older generation to a community of like-minded investors supporting the creation of meaningful partnerships.

6.7 Case Studies of SDGs Aligned Investments in Wealth Management

This case study illustrates a comprehensive integration of SDGs aligned investing within wealth management, combining real estate, private equity, liquid assets, family governance, active ownership, and philanthropy:

- Real estate and SDGs integration: The family's real estate holdings align with SDG 11 (Sustainable Cities) and SDG 6 (Clean Water). Investments target green-certified buildings to enhance energy efficiency, minimize environmental impact, and implement effective water management.
- Philanthropy aligned with SDGs: Through their foundation, the family supports SDG 4 (Quality Education) and SDG 3 (Good Health), amplifying their commitment to positive societal impact.
- Core and satellite liquid investments: The family's liquid portfolio includes a core multi-asset strategy for stability and a satellite portfolio for targeted SDGs exposure, focusing on SDG 7 (Clean Energy), SDG 9 (Innovation), and SDG 13 (Climate Action), balancing financial resilience with global sustainability goals.
- Thematic private equity for SDGs innovation: The family diversifies through a private equity fund focused on SDG 7 (Affordable Clean Energy) and SDG 9 (Innovation and Infrastructure). Using a blended finance model, this fund supports sustainable startups, de-risking impactful projects that might otherwise lack funding.
- Family governance and education: To maintain their SDGs aligned mission, the family organizes sessions with industry experts on sustainable investing and green technologies. Moreover, a family constitution reflects their commitment, ensuring all investment decisions align with shared values and sustainable principles.
- Active ownership: Through direct engagement with portfolio companies supported by a network of like-minded investors, the family promotes practices aligned with SDGs, such as diversity initiatives supporting SDG 5 (Gender Equality). This approach ensures their investments supports ethical priorities and meaningful contributions to global sustainability.

Integrating SDGs into wealth management enables wealth managers to guide high-net-worth individuals on their sustainability journey by connecting their investments to clear societal goals. It helps navigate the broad ESG landscape, ensuring alignment with investors' core values by focusing on specific SDGs that resonate with them.

References

Amundi.(2024). *2024 Responsible investment views*. Retrieved 20 November 2024, from https://research-center.amundi.com/files/nuxeo/dl/c7718ff0-16a9-41b0-a897-7e26f73b06ec?inline=.

Associazione Italiana Private Banking. (2022). *Response to the consultation on certain aspects of MiFID II suitability requirements of 27 January 2022 (ESMA35-43-2998)*. Retrieved November 20, 2024, from https://www.aipb.it/sites/default/files/all/2023-06/27%20APRILE%20 2022%20-%20ESMA%20-.%20RESPONSE%20CONSULTATION%20PAPER%20ON%20 GUIDELINES%20ON%20CERTAIN%20ASPECTS%20OF%20THE%20MIFID%20II%20 SUITABILITY%20REQUIREMENTS.pdf.

Australian Sustainable Finance Institute (ASFI). (2020). *Australian sustainable finance roadmap*. Retrieved 20, November, 2024 from https://static1.squarespace.com/static/6182172c8c1fdb1d7425fd0d/t/6240de97b51f1159dbc20e24/1648418477411/FINAL+Australian+Sustainable+Finance+Roadmap+%28mobile+version%29+%28Embargoed+until+24+November%29.pdf.

Auzepy, A., Bannier, C., & Gärtner, F. (2024). *Looking beyond ESG preferences: The role of sustainable finance literacy in sustainable investing* (Vol. 719, pp. 1–96). Center for Financial Studies.

Boston Consulting Group (BCG). (2022). *Sense and sustainability—global retail banking 2022*. Retrieved November 20, 2024, from https://web-assets.bcg.com/47/b0/0591daa24bf5a407385779fa374e/bcg-global-retail-banking-2022-sense-and-sustainability-sep-2022.pdf.

Bugg-Levine, A., & Emerson, J. (2011). Impact investing: Transforming how we make money while making a difference. *Innovations: Technology, Governance, Globalization, 6*(3), 9–18. Retrieved November 20, 2024. https://doi.org/10.1162/INOV_a_00077

Center for Sustainable Finance & Private Wealth of the University of Zurich. (CSP). (2022). *Sustainable investing capabilities of private banks*. Retrieved November 20, 2024, from: https://www.csp.uzh.ch/en/research/All-Publications/Sustainable-Investing-Capabilities-of-Private-Banks.html.

Cerulli Associates. (2022). *Cerulli anticipates $84 trillion in wealth transfers through 2045*. Retrieved November 20, 2024, from https://www.cerulli.com/press-releases/cerulli-anticipates-84-trillion-in-wealth-transfers-through-2045.

Dimson, E., Karakaş, O., & Li, X. (2015). Active ownership. *The Review of Financial Studies, 28*(12), 3225–3268. https://doi.org/10.1093/rfs/hhv044

Eccles, R. G., Lee, L.-E., & Stroehle, J. C. (2020). The social origins of ESG: An analysis of Innovest and KLD. *Organization & Environment, 33*(4), 575–596. Retrieved November 16, 2024, from https://www.jstor.org/stable/27001597

Elkington, J. (1997). *Cannibals with forks: The triple bottom line of 21st century business*. Capstone Publishing.

Ernst & Young (EY). (2023). *Global wealth research 2023*. Retrieved November 16, 2024, from https://assets.ey.com/content/dam/ey-sites/ey-com/en_gl/noindex/ey-2023-global-wealthresearch.pdf.

European Banking Authority (EBA). (2024). *Greenwashing monitoring and supervision: Final report*. Retrieved November 20, 2024, from https://www.eba.europa.eu/sites/default/files/2024-05/a12e5087-8fd2-451f-8005-6d45dc838ffd/Report%20on%20greenwashing%20 monitoring%20and%20supervision.pdf.

European Commission. (2018). *EU action plan on sustainable growth*. Retrieved November 22, 2024, from https://eur-lex.europa.eu/legal-content/EN/TXT/?uri=CELEX:52018DC0097.

European Union. (2017). Directive (EU) 2017/828 of the European Parliament and of the Council of 17 May 2017 amending Directive 2007/36/EC as regards the encouragement of long-term shareholder engagement (SRD II). *Official Journal of the European Union, L 132*, 1–25. Retrieved November 20, 2024, from https://eur-lex.europa.eu/legal-content/EN/TXT/?uri=CELEX:32017L0828

European Union. (2019). Regulation (EU) 2019/2088 of the European Parliament and of the Council of 27 November 2019 on sustainability-related disclosures in the financial services sector (SFDR). *Official Journal of the European Union, L 317*, 1–16. Retrieved November 20, 2024, from https://eur-lex.europa.eu/legal-content/EN/TXT/?uri=CELEX:32019R2088

European Union. (2020). Regulation (EU) 2020/852 of the European Parliament and of the Council of 18 June 2020 on the establishment of a framework to facilitate sustainable investment, and amending Regulation (EU) 2019/2088 (EU Taxonomy). *Official Journal of the European Union, L 198*, 13–43. Retrieved November 20, 2024, from https://eur-lex.europa.eu/legal-content/EN/TXT/?uri=CELEX:32020R0852

European Union. (2021). Directive (EU) 2021/338 of the European Parliament and of the Council of 16 February 2021 amending Directives 2014/65/EU on markets in financial instruments (MiFID II), and 2003/87/EC. *Official Journal of the European Union, L 68*, 14–27. Retrieved November 20, 2024, from https://eur-lex.europa.eu/legal-content/EN/TXT/?uri=CELEX:32021L0338

European Securities and Markets Authority (ESMA). (2024). *Final report—guidelines on funds's names using ESG or sustainability-related terms.* Retrieved November 22, 2024, from https://www.esma.europa.eu/sites/default/files/2024-05/ESMA34-472-440_Final_Report_Guidelines_on_funds_names.pdf.

Financial Conduct Authority (FCA). (2023). Policy Statement PS23/16 Sustainability Disclosure Requirements (SDR) and investment label. Retrieved November 22, 2024, from https://www.fca.org.uk/publication/policy/ps23-16.pdf.

Financial Reporting Council (FRC). (2020). *UK stewardship code 2020.* Retrieved November 20, 2024, from https://www.frc.org.uk/library/standards-codes-policy/stewardship/uk-stewardship-code/.

Financial Reporting Council (FCR). (2023). *FRC publishes research on impact of proxy advisers and ESG ratings agencies on companies and investors.* Retrieved November 22, 2024, from https://www.frc.org.uk/news-and-events/news/2023/06/frc-publishes-research-on-impact-of-proxy-advisers-and-esg-ratings-agencies-on-companies-and-investors/.

Financial Times. (2024). *Investors pull cash from ESG funds as performance lags.* Retrieved November 20, 2024, from https://www.ft.com/content/cf9001ab-e326-4264-af5e-12b3fbb0ee7b.

Financial Market Authority of Switzerland (FINMA). (2021). *FINMA guidance 05/2021—preventing and combating greenwashing.* Retrieved November 20, 2024, from https://www.finma.ch/en/~/media/finma/dokumente/dokumentencenter/myfinma/4dokumentation/finma-aufsichtsmitteilungen/20211103-finma-aufsichtsmitteilung-05-2021.pdf?sc_lang=en&hash=7F911020E829EA5910FF903AF851B2F3.

Forbes. (2022). *Gen Z disruption has just begun.* Retrieved November 20, 2024 from, https://www.forbes.com/sites/gregpetro/2022/02/18/gen-z-and-sustainability-the-disruption-has-only-just-begun/?sh=1a8e01503eb7.

Forbes. (2023). *Decoding the next generation of wealth owner the primal perspective*. Retrieved November 20, 2024, from https://www.forbes.com/sites/francoisbotha/2023/06/11/decoding-the-next-generation-of-wealth-owners-the-primal-perspective/.

Forum Nachhaltige Anlagen (FNG). (2022). *ESMA call for evidence on sustainability in suitability and product governance FNG response.* Retrieved November 20, 2024, from https://www.forum-ng.org/fileadmin/user_upload/ESMA_CfE_FNG_Response.pdf.

Global Impact Investing Network (GIIN). (2023). *Core characteristics of impact investing.* Retrieved November 16, 2024, from https://thegiin.org/publication/post/about-impact-investing/#what-is-impact-investing.

Global Investors for Sustainable Development (GISD) Alliance. (2020). *Sustainable development investing (SDI) definition.* Retrieved November 16, 2024, from https://www.gisdalliance.org/sites/default/files/2020-08/SDI%20Definition%20-%20Final%202020%2006%2004.pdf.

Hirst, S. (2016). Universal proxies. *Yale Journal on Regulation, 35*, 3–37. Discussion Paper No. 2016-11.

International Corporate Governance Network (ICGN). (2024). *Global stewardship guidelines*. Retrieved November 20, 2024, from https://www.icgn.org/sites/default/files/2024-10/ICGN%20Global%20Stewardship%20Principles%202024.pdf.

IMD. (2024). *Redefining wealth management: How family offices can lead the charge in responsible investing*. Retrieved November 16, 2024, from https://www.imd.org/ibyimd/finance/redefining-wealth-management-how-family-offices-can-lead-the-charge-in-responsible-investing-2/.

International Platform on Sustainable Finance (IPSF). (2024). *Stewardship and engagement in transition finance note*. Retrieved November 20, 2024, from https://finance.ec.europa.eu/document/download/22e45a45-85a8-4bc8-bcb1-fb0aa5f33e35_en?filename=241113-stewardship-and-engagement-in-transition-finance_en.pdf.

Katelouzou, D., & Puchniak, D. (2021). Global shareholder stewardship: Complexities, challenges, and possibilities. ECGI Law Working Paper, No. 595/202, 3–53.

Kölbel, J. & Weder, C. (2024). Sustainability preferences elicitation under MiFID II market study. University of St.Gallen Center for Financial Services Innovation. Retrieved November 20, 2024, from https://fsi.unisg.ch/fileadmin/user_upload/HSG_ROOT/Institut_FSI/Dokumente/Sustainable_Finance/Sustainability_Preference_Elicitation_Report.pdf.

Monetary Authority of Singapore (MAS). (2023). *Singapore-Asia taxonomy for sustainable finance*. Retrieved November 20, 2024, from https://www.mas.gov.sg/-/media/mas-media-library/development/sustainable-finance/singaporeasia-taxonomy-updated.pdf.

Monetary Authority of Singapore (MAS).(2022). *Disclosure and reporting guidelines for retail ESG funds*. Retrieved November 20, 2024, from https://www.mas.gov.sg/-/media/mas/regulations-and-financial-stability/regulations-guidance-and-licensing/securities-futures-and-fund-management/regulations-guidance-and-licensing/circulars/cfc-02-2022-disclosure-and-reporting-guidelines-for-retail-esg-funds.pdf.

Morgan Stanley. (2024a). *Sustainable signals—understanding individual investors' interests*. Retrieved November 20, 2024, from https://www.morganstanley.com/content/dam/msdotcom/en/assets/pdfs/MSInstituteforSustainableInvesting-SustainableSignals-Individuals-2024.pdf.

Morgan Stanley. (2024b). *Sustainable funds outperformed peers in 2023*. Retrieved November 20, 2024, from https://www.morganstanley.com/ideas/sustainable-funds-performance-2023-full-year.

Morgan Stanley. (2024c). *Sustainable reality*. Retrieved November 20, 2024, from https://www.morganstanley.com/content/dam/msdotcom/en/assets/pdfs/RO3865603-Sustainable_Reality_1H_2024_Report-FINAL.pdf.

Morningstar. (2024a). *Global sustainability fund flows Q3 2024 in review*. Retrieved November 20, 2024, from0 https://www.morningstar.com/lp/global-esg-flows.

Morningstar. (2024b). *What are sustainable funds and how have they performed*. Retrieved November 20, 2024, from https://www.morningstar.com/business/insights/blog/funds/us-sustainable-funds-performance.

NASDAQ. (2022). *How millennials and gen Z are driving growth behind ESG*. Retrieved November 22, from https://www.nasdaq.com/articles/how-millennials-and-gen-z-are-driving-growth-behind-esg. Accessed November 20, 2024

OECD. (2018). *Making blended finance work for the sustainable development goals*. OECD Publishing. https://doi.org/10.1787/9789264288768-en

OECD. (2020). *OECD business and finance outlook 2020: Sustainable and resilient finance*. OECD Publishing. https://doi.org/10.1787/eb61fd29-en

Päetzold, F., Ramiah, I., Rossi, M., & Weber, O. (2022). Between impact and returns: Private investors and the sustainable development goals. *Business Strategy and the Environment*. Retrieved November 16, 2024, from https://www.zora.uzh.ch/id/eprint/225308/1/Bus_Strat_Env___2022___Paetzold___Between_impact_and_returns_Private_investors_and_the_sustainable_development_goals.pdf

Renneboog, L., ter Horst, J., & Zhang, C. (2007). Socially responsible investments: Methodology, risk exposure, and performance. *European Corporate Governance Institute*. https://doi.org/10.2139/ssrn.985267

Securties and Exchange Commission (SEC). (2023). *Investment company names act*. Retrieved November 22, 2024, from https://www.sec.gov/files/rules/final/2023/33-11238.pdf.
Securities and Exchange Commission (SEC). (2019). *SEC clarifies investment advisers' proxy voting responsibilities and application of proxy rules to voting advice*. Retrieved November 22, 2024, from https://www.sec.gov/newsroom/press-releases/2019-158.
Swiss Banking Association. (2024). *Richtlinien für die Finanzdienstleister zum Einbezug von ESG-Präferenzen und ESG-Risiken und zur Prävention von Greenwashing bei der Anlageberatung und Vermögensverwaltung*. Retrieved November 22, 2024, from https://www.swissbanking.ch/_Resources/Persistent/2/8/7/5/287551ab09a651198fb8c7d6a62b4fc9ce3ca2af/SBVg_Richtlinien_Anlageberatung_und_Vermoegensverwaltung_DE_2024.pdf.
Swiss Federal Council. (2022). *Standpunkt des Bundesrates bezüglich Greenwashing Prävention im Finanzsektor*. Retrieved November 22, 2024, from https://www.newsd.admin.ch/newsd/message/attachments/74576.pdf.
Swiss Sustainable Finance (SSF). (2017). *Handbook on sustainable investments: Background information and practical examples for institutional asset owners*. CFA Institute Research.
Swiss Sustainable Finance (SSF). (2024). *Sustainable finance investment market study*. Retrieved November 20, 2024, from https://www.sustainablefinance.ch/api/rm/44H2452964U9V73/ssf-2024-ms-master-final-3.pdf.
Swiss Sustainable Finance (SSF) & Asset Management Association Switzerland (AMAS). (2023). Swiss Stewardship Code. Retrieved November 22, 2024, from https://www.sustainablefinance.ch/api/rm/5A7ME29CD6M925N/2023-10-04-swiss-stewardship-code-final.pdf.
United Nations. (2015). *Transforming our world: The 2030 agenda for sustainable development*. Retrieved November 16, 2024, from https://sdgs.un.org/goals.
United Nations Inter-agency Task Force on Financing for Development. (2024). F*inancing for sustainable development report 2024: Financing for development at a crossroads*. United Nations. Retrieved November 16, 2024, from https://financing.desa.un.org/iatf/report/financing-sustainable-development-report-2024.
UNTACT. (2024). *Sustainable finance trends 2023*. Retrieved November 22, 2024, from https://unctad.org/system/files/official-document/wir2024_ch03_en.pdf.
United Nations Principles on Responsible Investments (UN PRI). (2021). *Introduction to responsible stewardship*. Retrieved November 22, 2024, from https://www.unpri.org/download?ac=12686.
United Nations Principles on Responsible Investments (UN PRI). (2022). *Fiduciary duty in the 21st century—final report*. Retrieved November 22, 2024, from https://www.unpri.org/download?ac=9792.
Unites National Principles on Responsible Investments (UN PRI). (2018). *How ESG engagement creates value for investors and companies*. Retrieved November 16, 2024, from https://www.unpri.org/download?ac=4637.
United Nations Principles on Responsible Investments (UN PRI). (2024a). Retrieved November 22, 2024, from https://www.unpri.org/stewardship/about-stewardship/6268.article.
United Nations Principles on Responsible Investments (UN PRI). (2024b). *Corporate governance for asset owners*. Retrieved November 22, 2024, from https://www.unpri.org/download?ac=19880.
World Economic Forum. (2022). *Impact investing for next generations*. Retrieved November 22, 2024, from https://www3.weforum.org/docs/WEF_Impact_Investing_for_the_Next_Generation.pdf.

Chapter 7
Impact and Gender Lens Investing

Espinosa Arlette

7.1 Why Impact Investing?

In the words of the European Union High-Level Expert Group, sustainable finance is a stable financial system that tackles long-term education, economic, social, and environmental issues and integrates them into financial decisions (EU High-Level Expert Group, 2018). Following that term, and as mentioned previously in this book, sustainable investments integrate environmental, social, and governance considerations into selecting and managing investments (SSF, Swiss Sustainable Finance, 2020) to unchain long-term and sustainable value creation.

While sustainable investments have the same intrinsic purpose, there are differences between the manner, thematic(s), focus, and actual impacts that the several sustainable investment approaches result in. As classified in the last years, the nine main sustainability-driven investment strategies have been understood to be exclusion, best-in-class, norms-based screening, ESG integration, ESG engagement, thematic investment, and impact investing. However, in 2022, Eurosif, the University of Hamburg, and F.I.R.S.T. defined a further classification mapping the sophistication of the investment approaches and the impact they create. The proposed five categories include:

- Exclusion-focused investments,
- Basic ESG investments,
- Advanced ESG investments,
- Impact-aligned investments, and
- Impact-generating investments (Busch et al., 2022)

Why to further classify? Since the increasing rise of sustainability concerns, numerous sustainable investment products have been created, named, and advertised with

E. Arlette (✉)
Women In Sustainable Finance (WISF), Olten, Switzerland

K. Wendt, M. Ra (eds.), *Sustainable Wealth Management Revisited*, Sustainable Finance, https://doi.org/10.1007/978-3-032-02530-2_7

the promise of delivering a positive impact and contributing to sustainable development. However, as discussed in this book, many portfolios have shown discrepancies between their marketed philosophy and their real measurable impact. This phenomenon refers to the widespread concept of *greenwashing*, which means promoting false solutions to the climate crisis that distract from and delay concrete and credible action (UN, Greenwashing – the deceptive tactics behind environmental claims, 2022). This also applies to social and governance aspects of investment decisions.

To counter back greenwashing, actors in the sustainable finance ecosystem, including authorities, regulators, researchers, and other impact enablers, have developed knowledge and created further reporting frameworks, metrics, labels, and guidance on how to name funds, standardize practices, and have made clear classifications for investment products based on their impact. Here, the relevance of the categorization list shown above by Busch et al. (from Eurosif, Universität Hamburg, F.I.R.S.T.) supports the view that both impact-aligned and impact-generating approaches are the most concrete ways to deliver sustainable transition and growth above other approaches, at least when applied alone. For example, while investment exclusions- of harmful or unsustainable sectors- was one of the first approaches applied in the history of sustainable investments, now it results clear- as expressed by Swiss Sustainable Finance- that exclusions should not be taken as the only investment practice by sustainable investment managers, but as a screening or in conjunction with other practices when it comes to assessing investments (SSF, Swiss Sustainable Investment Market Study 2023, 2023).

7.2 The Concept of Impact Investing

The following subsections are dedicated to impact investments' general concepts and practices. As coined by the Global Impact Investing Network (GIIN, What you need to know about impact investing, 2023), impact investments are investments made to generate positive, measurable social and/or environmental impact alongside a financial return. Following five defined elements, impact investors incorporate:

1. The intentionality of pursuing positive social and/or environmental impact through investments,
2. Investment with financial return expectations,
3. Range of return expectations and asset classes, including but not limited to cash equivalents, fixed income, venture capital and private equity, and
4. Impact measurement is a commitment of the investor to measure and report the social and/or environmental performance and progress of underlying investments, ensuring transparency and accountability. (GIIN, What you need to know about impact investing, 2023)

It might be clear the difference between impact- as a sustainable approach- and traditional investing when comparing their main objectives, where impact investing has a sustainability objective. In contrast, traditional investing has a pure financial objective and not necessarily an intended sustainability one. However, for first-time audiences, impact investing could be confused with another financial mechanism, philanthropy, as both aim to generate impact in society and the environment. Nevertheless, we must remember from the before mentioned GIIN's definition that impact investing also pursues a financial return for the investors. Source: Own illustration.

7.3 Size and Market Characteristics of Impact Investing

From the GIIN's report "Sizing the Impact Investing Market 2024", about 3907 organizations currently manage 1.57 trillion USD in impact investing AUM worldwide, showing a 21% compound annual growth (CAGR) since 2019 (Hand et al., 2024a, 2024b). Following the GIIN's report, from a sample of 1593 impact investors worldwide, the average and median investment portfolios sum up to 986 and 42 million USD, respectively, showing apparent deviations between the size of the investment organizations. Furthermore, 45% of impact investors are located in Europe, 34% in the United States and Canada, and the rest is spread between Asia, Latin America, Africa, and the rest of the world. Finally, with data from the GSIA, impact investing is driven mainly by institutional investors with a 75% share of AUM.

But, how big is the impact investing market? By the end of 2023, the global sustainable investing AUM added up to 30.3 trillion USD (GSIA, 2023), while the global general investment market was valued at 128 trillion USD (Thinking Ahead Institute, 2024). Following those numbers, sustainable investments were around 24% of the global investment market, and impact investing accounts for 1.22% of international investments by 2023. In comparison, the Global Sustainable Investment Alliance (GSIA) has estimated that corporate engagement and shareholder action (accounting for 8.05 trillion USD), ESG integration (5.6 trillion USD), and negative screening/exclusions (3.8 trillion USD) are the most applied investment approaches when it comes to sustainability. At the same time, impact investing is the least applied approach, given the expertise needed in its application or the confusion between concepts. In the following subsections, we will untangle some of the practices that investors applying impact approaches take to construct strategies, aiming to clarify and inspire practitioners to develop such impactful investments. The ultimate purpose is to help the impact ecosystem further develop and unleash impact market potential.

7.4 Impact Investment Themes

Certainly, impact investing has a lot of variety in terms of the sectors and business models in which investors can focus capital. One way to classify the topics is by pairing them with the United Nations' SDGs (UN, 2015) that they relate to. The figure below shows a list of the common impact sector topics, and it is constructed with data from the UN, the Private Asset Impact Fund Report 2022 from Tameo (2022) and the insights from Phenix Capital (2024), both well-recognized research organizations in the impact investing area (Fig. 7.1).

Sustainable Development Goal	Investment Sectors or Themes
SDG 1: No Poverty	- Financial inclusion - Microfinance
SDG 2: Zero Hunger	- Sustainable agriculture - Sustainable farming - Solutions and financing for small agriculture and farming producers - Food technologies
SDG 3: Good Health and Well-being	- Healthcare - Biotech - Longevity - Well-being
SDG 4: Quality Education	- Accessible education solutions - Educational technologies
SDG 5: Gender Equality	- Gender lens investing (GLI)
SDG 6: Clean Water and Sanitation	- Water Utilities - Water sanitation technologies - Water efficiency technologies
SDG 7: Affordable and Clean Water	- Renewable energy - Energy efficiency technologies - Energy solutions for inaccessible geographical populations
SDG 8: Decent Work and Economic Growth	- Training and skill development solutions - Advising companies - Labor market placement platforms

Fig. 7.1 Impact investment themes by SDG. Source: Own illustration

SDG 9: Industry, Innovation and Infrastructure	- FinTech - Accessible IT solutions
SDG 10: Reduce Inequalities	- Solutions directed to increase inclusion of overall groups into society
SDG 11: Sustainable Cities and Communities	- Clean transport - Affordable housing - Green buildings - Green infrastructure - Smart city technologies
SDG 12: Responsible Consumption and Production	- Waste management - Ethical products production - Sustainable supply chain
SDG 13: Climate Action	- Climate mitigation solutions - Climate adaptation solutions
SDG 14: Life Below Water	- Sustainable aquaculture - Sustainable fisheries - Ocean restoration and preservation solutions and projects
SDG 15: Life on Land	- Forestry management solutions - Biodiversity conservation projects and technologies - Ecosystem restoration projects and solutions

Fig. 7.1 (continued)

7.5 Creation and Management of Impact Investing Strategies

One of the most critical pieces of guidance available for impact investors and industry practitioners pursuing the creation of impactful strategies is the Operating Principles for Impact Management created by the International Finance Corporation (IFC). The principles are a set of best practices for impact investing incorporating and assessing impact all along the investment creation and process, departing from the drafting of investment strategic intent, the origination, and structuring of investments, the portfolio management phase, until the exit of investments (IFC, 2019).

The nine IFC Impact Principles follow more or less the same process as a traditional investment manager would to create an investment product (especially private investors), select investments, track the financial performance, and exit the investment, either by selling the assets in the case of listed companies, or bonds or by exiting private equity and debt investments. The key concept added by the IFC via the nine principles, is the impact element at all steps of the definition and investment process, from the design and management of the impact objectives, assessment and monitoring of the impact results, lessons learned, and the provision of an independent verification. As for the last concept on independent verification, this refers to verifying the positive and negative impact generated during an investment, and it is performed by a third-party organization dedicated to measuring, tracking, and assessing discrepancies in the impact generated by the investee and investor. Some examples of independent verification providers are Tameo, Phenix Capital, BlueMark, and EDGE.

Finally, and harmonically conveying the impact principles, back in 2019, the GIIN published the Core Characteristics of Impact Investing, which also emphasize best practices guiding impact investors to creating and managing investment products. The GIIN Core Characteristics include:

- Drive investment with intentionality and desire to contribute to measurable social or environmental benefit,
- Use evidence and impact data in investment design,
- Manage impact performance while communicating performance and feedback information to support the investment impact management, and
- Contribute to the Impact Industry's growth by applying credible impact investing practices and shared industry terms, conventions, and indicators (GIIN, Core Characteristics of Impact Investing, 2019).

7.6 Impact Measurement and Management

Note that reporting regulations and frameworks are not covered in this chapter as they are discussed extensively in previous sections of the book. Nevertheless, when it comes to impact investing, it is highly relevant to discuss the practices, indicators, and metrics used for impact measurement and assessment, as impact investing flags precisely that: tracking impact clearly. Given that the impact investment approach focuses on genuinely sustainable sectors and businesses, one can root the metrics and track impact based on the most critical sustainability guidance, which is the UN's SDGs. So, as a final reflection on impact investing, we discuss two essential considerations: the five dimensions of impact by the Impact Management Project (IMP) and the IRIS+ (2024) impact metrics.

In 2021, the Impact Management Project (IMP), in partnership with IRIS+ (2024), gathered and defined knowledge on measuring, assessing, and reporting both companies' and investments' impacts. As a result, the IMP originally defined the five dimensions of impact as follows:

- WHAT the outcomes the investee/enterprise contribute to, and how important it is for those stakeholders.
- WHO the stakeholders experiencing the effect are.
- HOW MUCH the outcome for stakeholders is in terms of scale, depth and duration.
- CONTRIBUTION in terms of the outcome contribution depth while producing impact.
- RISK being seen as the likelihood that the impact would be different than expected (IMP & IRIS+, 2020).

Finally, and to reconvene in the metrics impact investors use to track the impact- and assess the five dimensions- a widely used set is the GIIN's IRIS+ Core Metrics Sets, where the complete list is available on the IRIS Catalog of Metrics site, classified and adapted for better usability of impact investors. While the list of metrics is not disclosed in this chapter, the main branch classifications of the IRIS+ (2024) metrics are done by:

- Impact Category or Topic
- SDG focus
- Dimensions of Impact
- Investment Lens, etc.

7.7 The Gender Lens Investing Case

As a practical example, the next subsections focus on digging in one very relevant topic for world's sustainability, but yet not enough funded impact investment theme, the Gender Lens Investing. It is well-known there are several areas where gender-based inequalities are present worldwide. Firstly, one of the most relevant references can be found in the United Nations Development Program (UNDP) who measures and produces the Gender Inequality Index (GII) evaluating gender-based disadvantages in three dimensions: reproductive health, empowerment, and labor market participation (UNDP, 2024), and comparing the state of those variables on a country-development level. As per the historical index values of the GII, for countries with low human development- on average- the index shows higher inequality levels when compared to high human development countries. For example, in the area of female reproductive health issues, less developed countries show higher maternity mortality and the adolescent birth rates. In contrast, when it comes to empowerment, we see similar levels of inequality across countries, where women have less representation in the political sphere worldwide.

When we look at the state of gender equality at the corporate level, based on studies from Equileap, the share of female versus male workforce across industries also shows inequalities at the five workforce levels: base workforce, senior management positions, executives, board members, and ultimately, the CEO. It is observed that the participation of women decreases the higher the position level we look at. For the basis of the pyramid, the primary workforce, women and men, have a close share of positions, 40% female workers versus 60% male employees. However, when we move above into senior management, from 100% of the positions, only 25% of senior managers are women versus 75% of men. Moreover, all the way to the top, from 100% of CEOs per country average, only 6% are female (Equileap, 2023).

Lastly, the worldwide gender pay gap was equivalent to 20% by the end of 2023 (UN Women, 2024). The pay gap is defined as the difference between the salary a woman receives for a job and the salary a man receives for performing that job.

To contribute to decrease the gender gap, the Criterion Institute has defined Gender Lens Investing (GLI) as an approach that incorporates a gender analysis into financial analysis to get better outcomes for investors, businesses, and most importantly, society (Criterion Institute, 2015). At a glance, GLI focuses on redirecting capital to promote gender equality. To achieve this objective, investors must take gender-based considerations across the investment process, focusing on innovative and catalyst women-led efforts and solutions focused on achieving gender equality at the workplace, supporting female entrepreneurs and developing products and services that empower women and girls.

Regarding the GLI market depth, Parallele Finance estimates that by the second quarter of 2024, a total of USD 4.61 billion were invested in publicly traded Gender Lens Equity Funds (GLEFs) (Parallele Finance, 2024). On the side of private investments, 2X Global and Sagana's Project Catalyst report estimates that by the end of 2023, private funds with a gender lens summed a total of USD 7.9 USD in AUM (2X Global & Sagana, Project Catalyst, 2024).

7.7.1 Filtering Gender Lens Businesses and Measuring Impact

In 2018, 2X Challenge- an initiative encouraging investors around the globe to redirect capital into businesses supporting gender equality- launched the now widely used gender lens investing standard called the 2X Criteria (2X Challenge, 2024). Firstly, the 2X Criteria helps investors streamline, assess, and select companies with missions, products, or practices working towards gender equality. Secondly, investors use the criteria to track and periodically report the advancements and gender-based impact created by the invested companies. The first version of the 2X Criteria was a set of minimum one-fits-all-sectors requirements. However, it was revised in June 2024 to incorporate sector and country-based considerations to better account for historical differences in gender equality practices in both layers. As presented in the figure below, the 2X Criteria help investors to visualize companies with gender lens characteristics, where if a company fulfills one or more of the following criteria, it is considered eligible for gender lens investment prior to further assessment (Fig. 7.2).

On the reporting side, investors- especially the ones in impact investing- use the GIIN's IRIS+ (2024) indicators adapted to the 2X criteria. The indicators comprise: percent of female ownership, percent of company founder(s) who are female, percent of senior management who are female, percent of Board who are female, percent of ICs who are female, percent of employees (FTE) who are female, investee has the initiative in place to specifically advance women in the workforce (Y/N), investee's product or service specifically or disproportionately benefits women (Y/N), percent of customers who are female, share of Fund's portfolio that meets at least one of the direct 2X criteria, and share of Fund's portfolio that meets at least one of the direct 2X criteria. (IRIS+, IRIS+ and 2X Challenge, 2019).

7.7.2 Gender Lens Investing Process

In the investment world, several possibilities exist for managing investment portfolios in wholesale and individual wealth management. This, of course, applies to GLI as well when it comes to defining the investment philosophy, designing and implementing the investment process and how gender lens considerations are incorporated, tracking and reporting impact metrics, and selecting and implementing tools, programs, and practices applied along the investment cycle. In the case of GLI, when an investment manager implements a strategy, the most common practice is to incorporate gender goals in the investment thesis, and going further, to analyze pipeline companies and portfolio companies during the investment assessment. We can depict a straightforward yet encompassing investment process inspired by the guidance of 2X Global toolkits, and the best practices from the IMP and GIIN. The next process takes the example of what a private investing manager would do:

Step 1: Screening of potential investees. Assess companies both in their business models, financials, and how they perform with regards to the 2X Challenge and IRIS+ metrics. This analysis can be conducted with interviews and questionnaires with the company for private investments or analyzing published data for listed investments.

Step 2: Negotiation and deal structuring. Taking into account the results of the company gender assessment, the investment managers- together with the investee- stipulate goals for the investees to advance in its gender practices and the development of products that support women and girls, and commit to gender metrics to follow up and report the advancements.

2X Criteria	Threshold
1. Entrepreneurship & Ownership	
Share of women's ownership, or	Equal or greater than 51%
Business is founded by a woman	Equal or greater than 50%
2. Leadership	
Share of women in senior management, or	Varies according to country & sector specific thresholds
Share of women on the Board or Investment Committee	Varies according to country & sector specific thresholds
3. Employment	
Share of women in the workforce	Varies according to country & sector specific thresholds
One quality employment indicator beyond compliance	Yes/No
4. Supply chain	
Commitment to women in the supply chain, and	Yes/No
One quality supply chain indicator beyond compliance	Yes/No
5. Products & services	
Product empowers women and girls and enhances their well-being and equity or	Yes/No
Service empowers women and girls and enhances their well-being and equity	Yes/No
6. Portfolio	
Investments through financial intermediaries aligned with the 2X Criteria	

Fig. 7.2 2X criteria for gender lens investing selection and assessment. Source: Own representation

Step 3: Approval and Investment. The portfolio accepts or rejects investments based on the results of the gender metrics assessment and the companies' commitments to improving their gender practices.

Step 4: Tracking Impact and Portfolio Performance. As with all sustainable investing approaches and themes, gathering data, measuring, tracking, and monitoring gender equality metrics is important to assess whether the investees have improved during the investment period and follow regulation reporting.

Step 5: Exit. While exiting an investment, investors assess the companies' final performance and gender metrics and evaluate whether impact was created, and whether initial goals were achieved.

7.7.3 Technical Assistance

Finally, to advance the gender practices of investees, an investment management company can offer as well technical assistance to develop companies' capabilities and capacity. A simple list of the steps performed during technical assistance programs following the knowledge of Value for Women (n.d.) may include:

1. Gender assessment of pipeline and portfolio companies, using interviews, discussions, field visits, and questionnaires to assess their gender practices in the organizational culture.
2. Analysis of the information gathered during the assessment. In this phase, the investor also calculates gender lens metrics.
3. The investment manager produces and discusses recommendations and action plans with the investee, projects are directed to help the companies to pursue gender equality impact.
4. A strategy and work plan are designed based on the gender lens projects the investee agrees to work on with the manager.
5. Continuous measurement of the progress and gender lens metrics based on the action plan results.
6. Evaluation of the program results and final recommendations.

Note that the investment manager measures the impact created during the technical assistance program, not only during steps 1 and 6 but also throughout the entire process. Common metrics are those from the already mentioned 2X criteria and the IRIS+. Furthermore, the investment manager can proportionate the technical assistance either using their own infrastructure and knowledge or through another actor, such as a foundation.

References

2X Challenge. (2024, 09 30). *2X criteria*. Retrieved from 2x Challenge: https://www.2xchallenge.org/2xcriteria.

2X Global. (2024). JEDI investing toolkit. Retrieved from JEDI Investing: https://jediinvesting.com/.

2X Global, & Sagana. (2024). *Project catalyst*. 2X Global and Sagana.

Busch, T., Stapelfeldt, M., van Hoorn, V., & Pruessner, E. (2022). *Classification scheme for sustainable investments*. Eurosif, Universität Hamburg, F.I.R.S.T.

Criterion Institute. (2015). *White paper: How to upgrade your due diligence with a gender lens*. Criterion Institute.

Equileap. (2023). Gender equality global report and ranking. Equileap. Retrieved from https://equileap.com/wp-content/uploads/2024/04/Equileap_2024_Gender_Equality_Report_Emerging_Markets.pdf.

EU High-Level Expert Group. (2018). *Financing a sustainable European economy*. Retrieved from sustainable finance final report. https://finance.ec.europa.eu/system/files/2018-01/180131-sustainable-finance-final-report_en.pdf.

GIIN. (2019, 4 3). Core Characteristics of Impact Investing. Retrieved from The GIIN: https://s3.amazonaws.com/giin-web-assets/giin/assets/publication/post/core-characteristics-webfile.pdf.

GIIN. (2023, 01 01). What you need to know about impact investing. Retrieved from The GIIN: https://thegiin.org/publication/post/about-impact-investing/#what-is-impact-investing.

GSIA. (2023). *Global sustainable investment review 2023*. Retrieved from Global Sustainable Investment Alliance: https://www.gsi-alliance.org/global-sustainable-investment-review-finds-us30-trillion-invested-in-sustainable-assets/.

Hand, D., Sunderji, S., Ulanow, M., Remsberg, R., & Xi. (2024a). *IN FOCUS: Gender and impact investing in 2024*. Global Impact Investing Network (GIIN).

Hand, D., Xiao, K., Ulanow, M., & Pan, H. (2024b). *Sizing the impact investing market 2024*. The Global Impact Investing Network. Retrieved from https://s3.amazonaws.com/giin-web-assets/giin/assets/publication/giin-sizingtheimpactinvestingmarket-2024.pdf.

IFC. (2019). *Impact principles*. Retrieved from IFC: https://www.impactprinciples.org/9-principles.

IMP, & IRIS+. (2020). *IRIS+ Five dimensions of impact*. Retrieved from IRIS+: https://s3.amazonaws.com/giin-web-assets/iris/assets/files/guidance/IRIS-five-dimensions_June-2020.

IRIS+. (2019). *IRIS+ and 2X challenge*. Retrieved from The GIIN: https://iris.thegiin.org/document/iris-and-2x-challenge/.

IRIS+. (2024). *IRIS catalog of metrics*. Retrieved from The GIIN: https://iris.thegiin.org/metrics/.

Parallele Finance. (2024). Gender lens investing (GLI) Q2 2024. Parallele FInance. Retrieved from https://parallellefinance.com/gli-q2-2024/.

Phenix Capital. (2024). *Sustainable development goals & impact investing themes*. Retrieved from Phenix Capital: https://phenixcapitalgroup.com/sustainable-development-goals-impact-investing-themes.

SSF. (2020). *Swiss sustainable finance*. Retrieved from SSF Module 1: https://www.sustainablefinance.ch/elearning/SSF_Module1_EN/story.html.

SSF. (2023). *Swiss sustainable investment market study 2023*. Swiss Sustainable Finance.

Tameo. (2022). *Private assets Impact fund report 2022*. Tameo.

Thinking Ahead Institute. (2024, October 17). Retrieved from Thinking Ahead Institute: https://www.thinkingaheadinstitute.org/news/article/worlds-largest-investment-managers-see-assets-hit-128-trillion-in-return-to-growth/

UN. (2022). Greenwashing—the deceptive tactics behind environmental claims. Retrieved from United Nations: https://www.un.org/en/climatechange/science/climateissues/greenwashing

UN Women. (2024, 2 22). Everything you need to know about pushing for pay equity. Retrieved from UN Women: https://www.unwomen.org/en/news/stories/2020/9/explainer-everything-you-need-to-know-about-equal-pay.
UNDP. (2024). Retrieved from Gender Development Index: https://hdr.undp.org/gender-development-index#/indicies/GDI.
United Nations. (2015). *Sustainable development goals*. Retrieved from United Nations: https://sdgs.un.org/goals.
Value for Women. (n.d.). Our work. Retrieved from Value for Women: https://www.v4w.org/work.

Chapter 8
Longevity Finance: A Gender-Specific Approach

Karen Wendt and Marta Ra

8.1 Introduction to Longevity Finance

Longevity Finance refers to financial strategies, products, and services designed to address the financial needs of individuals as they age, particularly in the context of increasing life expectancy. This concept is becoming increasingly relevant as global populations age and retirement periods extend. However, the financial implications of longevity are not gender-neutral. Women, on average, live longer than men but face unique challenges that necessitate a gender-specific approach.

Key factors driving the need for a gender-specific approach include:

Longer Lifespans: Women tend to outlive men by 5–7 years on average, leading to greater healthcare and retirement costs (World Health Organization, 2021; United Nations, 2020; National Institute on Aging, 2020).

Economic Disparities: Women often earn less than men over their lifetimes due to wage gaps, career breaks for caregiving, and part-time work (OECD, 2020; International Labour Organization, 2021; UN Women, 2022).

Financial Literacy Gap: Studies show that women often report lower levels of confidence in financial planning and investment decisions compared to men (Lusardi & Mitchell, 2014; McKinsey & Company, 2021; PricewaterhouseCoopers, 2021).

K. Wendt
President Sustainable Finance, Eccos Impact GmbH, Cham, Switzerland
e-mail: karen@sustainablefinance.io

M. Ra (✉)
Women In Sustainable Finance (WISF), Zurich, Switzerland
e-mail: marta.ra@wisfinternational.com

K. Wendt, M. Ra (eds.), *Sustainable Wealth Management Revisited*, Sustainable Finance, https://doi.org/10.1007/978-3-032-02530-2_8

Cultural Expectations: Women are more likely to serve as caregivers for children and elderly family members, which impacts their ability to save for retirement (National Alliance for Caregiving, 2021; OECD, 2020; UN Women, 2022).

This chapter explores how financial solutions can address these gender-specific challenges and promote financial security for women throughout their extended lifespans.

8.2 Demographic Trends and Their Impact

Global demographic trends highlight the need for targeted longevity finance strategies. These trends include:

Aging Populations: By 2050, the number of people aged 60 and older is expected to double, with women comprising a larger proportion of this demographic (United Nations, 2020; European Commission, 2021; World Bank, 2022). Longer lifespans mean women are more likely to experience periods of financial dependency in old age.

Regional Variations: In developed economies, women often retire earlier but live longer, creating a longer retirement phase with inadequate savings (OECD, 2020; International Labour Organization, 2021; United Nations, 2020).

In developing economies, women face limited access to formal financial systems and are more reliant on informal savings mechanisms (World Bank, 2022; Grameen Foundation, 2020; UN Women, 2022).

Caregiving Responsibilities: Women often assume caregiving roles, which can result in career interruptions, lower lifetime earnings, and reduced retirement contributions (National Alliance for Caregiving, 2021; OECD, 2020; UN Women, 2022).

Health Disparities: Women experience higher healthcare costs in old age due to longer lifespans and greater susceptibility to chronic conditions such as osteoporosis and dementia (National Institute on Aging, 2020; World Health Organization, 2021; Kaiser Family Foundation, 2022).

The intersection of these trends underscores the importance of creating financial solutions that address women's unique challenges while leveraging their longer lifespans as an opportunity for extended economic participation.

8.3 Financial Products and Services for Longevity

Existing financial products often fail to consider the specific needs of women, particularly as they age. A gender-specific approach to longevity finance could include the following innovations:

8.3.1 *Insurance Products*

Long-Term Care Insurance Policies that account for women's higher likelihood of requiring long-term care services (American Association for Long-Term Care Insurance, 2021; Kaiser Family Foundation, 2022; Deloitte, 2022).

Health Insurance Comprehensive plans covering gender-specific health needs, including post-menopausal care and chronic conditions (World Health Organization, 2021; Kaiser Family Foundation, 2022; UN Women, 2022).

8.3.2 *Retirement Planning Tools*

Pension Schemes Flexible pension plans that allow for contributions during career breaks or caregiving periods (International Labour Organization, 2021; OECD, 2020; McKinsey & Company, 2021).

Spousal Benefits Policies that enable women to benefit from a partner's retirement plan, particularly in economies where gender pay gaps are significant (OECD, 2020; UN Women, 2022; European Commission, 2021).

8.3.3 *Investment Opportunities*

Women-Focused Funds Investment products that prioritize women-led businesses or initiatives aligned with gender equality (Morningstar, 2021; PricewaterhouseCoopers, 2021; TechCrunch, 2022).

Longevity Bonds Financial instruments designed to provide stable income streams over extended retirement periods (European Investment Bank, 2021; McKinsey & Company, 2021; OECD, 2020).

8.3.4 *Access to Financial Education*

Programs aimed at improving women's financial literacy and investment confidence (Lusardi & Mitchell, 2014; UN Women, 2022; Grameen Foundation, 2020).

Community-based initiatives to teach financial planning in underserved areas (Grameen Foundation, 2020; UN Women, 2022; Morningstar, 2021).

Addressing barriers to access, such as limited control over household finances or lack of identification for opening accounts, is critical in ensuring these solutions are effective.

8.4 Technology and Innovation

Advancements in technology are transforming the landscape of longevity finance, offering new opportunities to address women's unique financial needs:

8.4.1 Fintech Solutions

Digital Savings Platforms Apps that help women save and invest, often with features tailored to their goals and timelines (PricewaterhouseCoopers, 2021; Grameen Foundation, 2020; TechCrunch, 2022).

Microfinance Platforms Digital solutions enabling women in developing countries to access credit and build financial independence (Grameen Foundation, 2020; UN Women, 2022; McKinsey & Company, 2021).

8.4.2 Artificial Intelligence and Big Data

Personalized Financial Planning AI-driven tools that provide tailored advice based on individual health, career, and financial profiles (Accenture, 2021; Deloitte, 2022; McKinsey & Company, 2021).

Predictive Analytics Tools that assess longevity risks and recommend optimal savings and investment strategies (McKinsey & Company, 2021; European Investment Bank, 2021; PricewaterhouseCoopers, 2021).

8.4.3 Health-Tech Innovations

Wearable Devices Technologies that monitor health and provide data to inform insurance underwriting and financial planning (Deloitte, 2022; National Institute on Aging, 2020; Frost & Sullivan, 2021).

Biotech Advancements Innovations that improve longevity and quality of life, requiring financial products to support extended active years (Frost & Sullivan, 2021; World Health Organization, 2021; Accenture, 2021).

8.4.4 Startups Focused on Women

Highlight examples such as platforms offering women-centric financial literacy programs or investment apps designed specifically for women (TechCrunch, 2022; Morningstar, 2021; PricewaterhouseCoopers, 2021).

8.5 Conclusion

A gender-specific approach to longevity finance is essential for addressing the unique challenges women face as they age. By leveraging demographic insights, creating tailored financial products, and harnessing technology, we can build a more inclusive financial ecosystem that empowers women to achieve financial security and independence throughout their extended lifespans.

References

Accenture. (2021). *The future of AI in financial planning*. American Association for Long-Term Care Insurance. (2021). *Long-term care trends.*
American Association for Long-Term Care Insurance. (2021). Long-Term Care Insurance price index. American Association for Long-Term Care Insurance. https://www.aaltci.org/long-term-care-insurance/learning-center/ltcfacts-2021.php
Deloitte. (2022). *The role of wearable technology in healthcare.*
European Commission. (2021). Women and retirement in Europe.
European Investment Bank. (2021). *Longevity bonds: An innovative financial instrument.*
Frost & Sullivan. (2021). *Biotech innovations for aging populations.*
Grameen Foundation. (2020). *Digital microfinance solutions for women.*
International Labour Organization (ILO). (2021). *Gender-responsive pension systems.*
Kaiser Family Foundation. (2022). *Health insurance and gender disparities.*
Lusardi, A., & Mitchell, O. S. (2014). Financial literacy and financial planning: Evidence from global data. *Journal of Pension Economics & Finance, 13*(4), 497–508. https://doi.org/10.1017/S1474747214000032
McKinsey & Company. (2021). *Predictive analytics in longevity finance.*
Morningstar. (2021). *Investing in gender equality: Women-focused funds.*
National Alliance for Caregiving. (2021). *Caregiving in the U.S.*
National Institute on Aging. (2020). *Women and aging: Health challenges.*
Organisation for Economic Co-operation and Development (OECD). (2020). *Gender and pensions.*
PricewaterhouseCoopers (PwC). (2021). *The rise of fintech solutions for women.*
TechCrunch. (2022). *Startups empowering women in finance.*

UN Women. (2022). *The gender implications of caregiving.*
United Nations. (2020). *World population aging report.*
World Bank. (2022). *Financial inclusion and women.*
World Health Organization (WHO). (2021). *Global health and life expectancy trends.*

Chapter 9
Artificial Intelligence in Wealth Management

Sabrina Herold and Christina Goltzsche

9.1 Introduction to Artificial Intelligence

This section aims to equip the reader with foundational concepts in artificial intelligence and provide an overview of its history.

9.1.1 Foundational Concepts and Terminology

The term "artificial intelligence" was officially coined in 1956 at the Dartmouth Conference, marking the formal establishment of AI as an academic discipline. The following concepts are of relevance to the subject at hand today:

Artificial intelligence (AI) refers to the theory and development of computer systems designed to perform tasks traditionally requiring human intelligence. These tasks include reasoning, problem-solving, learning, perception, language understanding, pattern identification and decision-making (Russel & Norvig, 2021). AI serves as an overarching concept that encompasses a broad range of technologies, including machine learning, deep learning, and generative artificial intelligence (Fig. 9.1).

Machine learning (ML) is a discipline within the field of AI. It focuses on the development, analysis, and implementation of statistical algorithms, commonly referred to as learning algorithms. These learning algorithms can learn from data. One distinguishes typically three kinds of learning paradigms: supervised,

S. Herold (✉)
The Singularity Group, Zurich, Switzerland
e-mail: sh@singularity-group.com

C. Goltzsche
LGT Bank (Schweiz) AG, Zurich, Switzerland

K. Wendt, M. Ra (eds.), *Sustainable Wealth Management Revisited*, Sustainable Finance, https://doi.org/10.1007/978-3-032-02530-2_9

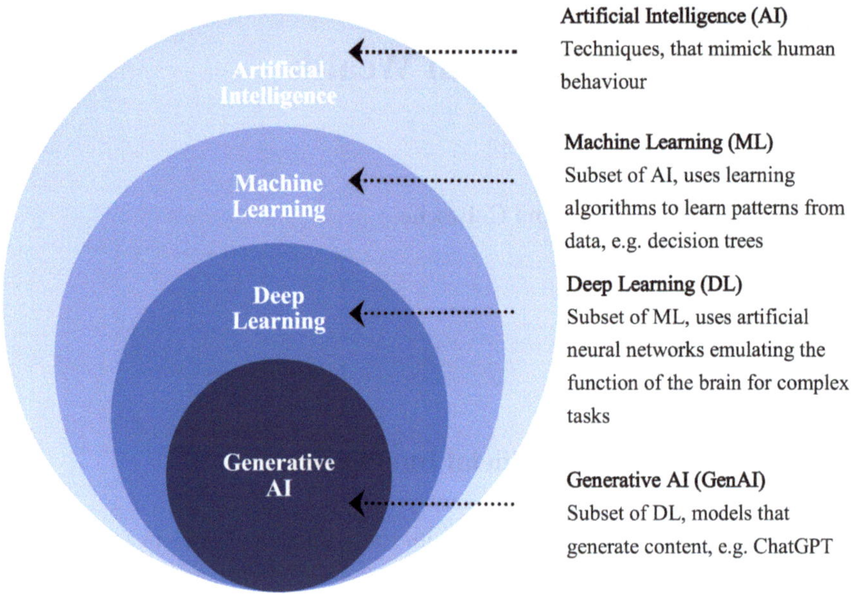

Fig. 9.1 Comparative overview of AI and its subfields, source: own illustration

unsupervised, and reinforcement learning. In supervised learning, the correct output for a given input is known, and the system learns a general rule by comparing the actual output to the desired output, aiming to minimize the error (Rojas, 1996). Unsupervised learning does not require known outputs, and the system learns based on the structure of the input data, often to identify patterns or clusters. Reinforcement learning represents a third category of learning paradigms, where the system learns through continuous interaction with the environment by receiving rewards or penalties. ML encompasses a wide variety of methods and algorithms, including techniques such as decision trees (Quinlan, 1986), k-means clustering (Lloyd, 1982) and support vector machines (Cortes & Vapnik, 1995), which are highly effective for predictive analytics and decision-making. These methods, while not based on neural networks, are critical components of the machine learning toolkit and demonstrate the breadth of the field.

Deep learning (DL), a subfield of ML, focuses on the use of artificial neural networks designed to simulate the structure and function of the human brain (Haykin, 1999). Artificial neural networks are composed of interconnected nodes that resemble neurons and synapses in a biological neural system. The connections between the neural network's nodes are weighted, and these weights are referred to as parameters. Learning algorithms are applied to "train" the artificial neural network to fulfill a certain task. The learning process typically begins with a randomly connected artificial neural network and throughout the learning process, connections between the artificial neurons are changed in order to get a rewired artificial neural network that correctly fulfills the task. These networks can have multiple layers mimicking the highly complex structure of the brain.

Generative artificial intelligence (GenAI) is a branch of AI, which can generate new content by extending or adapting existing data. These systems can produce text, language, images, music, and code. One example in this category are large language models (LLMs), which focus on language understanding and generation. Other examples in the area of image generation include Midjourney and DALL-E. Such models are typically based on DL architectures and have been trained with massive amounts of unlabeled data. While traditional AI is focused on tasks like analysis and prediction, GenAI is concerned with more creative tasks. LLMs allow individuals, including those without technical expertise, to interact effortlessly with the LLM by formulating prompts and utilizing the generated output. This accessibility contributed to a significant surge in popularity and extensive media attention. Moreover, generically trained LLMs can be finetuned and reused for many new computational and analytical tasks.

9.1.2 Historical Overview

The groundwork for AI was established by the pioneering figures of computing in the nineteenth century, most notably Ada Lovelace (Isaacson, 2014). The origins of AI itself date back to 1950 with Alan Turing's seminal paper, where he posed the question "can machines think?" and introduced the Turing Test to evaluate machine intelligence (Turing, 1950). AI entered the financial industry in 1982 with the foundation of the quant investment firm "Renaissance Technologies" by James Simons, marking a cornerstone in financial innovation. However, it was only in recent years that advances in computational power and the availability of massive data for training made it feasible to put AI, particularly DL, into widespread use. This surge in resources enabled the development of today's LLMs. Google's paper "Attention is all you need" (Vaswani et al., 2017), published in 2017, laid the foundation for the development of LLMs, such as GPT and BERT. Only a few years later, in 2020, the AI boom started with the appearance of LLMs, such as OpenAI's release of GPT-3 in 2020 with 175 bn parameters. Later, in November 2022 OpenAI released its new version GPT-3.5, known as ChatGPT, to the public. The browser-based release of ChatGPT enabled widespread access to LLMs.

To effectively leverage AI, wealth managers need to develop a comprehensive data strategy that includes investing in robust data infrastructure for collection, storage, processing, and management. Ensuring high data quality, implementing strong governance frameworks, and fostering cross-functional collaboration among quant analysts, IT professionals and business leaders are essential for aligning AI initiatives with strategic goals (Caserta et al., 2023).

9.2 Portfolio Management Supported by Artificial Intelligence

This subchapter explores the transformative role of AI in portfolio management, beginning with its application in enhancing traditional methods for asset return and risk estimation, and extending to its use in advanced optimization techniques, sustainability-focused investments, and emerging capabilities powered by LLMs.

9.2.1 AI-Enhanced Portfolio Construction

Constructing client portfolios by incorporating typical client needs, such as a long-term and steady growth of their assets, is at the core of wealth management and a familiar challenge for every portfolio manager. Portfolios are usually constructed based on the portfolio manager's views and forecasts of asset returns and risks. In order to construct portfolios, the mean variance optimization framework (MVO) as introduced by Markowitz (1952) is the industry standard. However, this approach has its pitfalls. One problem with this approach is that the resulting portfolio is very sensitive to the input data, i.e. the estimates of future expected asset returns and asset covariances (which measure how different asset prices move in relation to each other). Thus, estimating expected returns as well as asset covariances with sufficient accuracy poses a significant challenge.

AI can help to overcome such pitfalls by providing better estimates of asset returns and covariances. When it comes to stock return predictions, ML methods, particularly decision trees (models that use a tree-like structure to make decisions based on input features) and neural networks, outperform more traditional models as has been shown in a study by Gu et al. (2020). This superior performance is because these ML methods can capture nonlinear relationships between predictor variables, which traditional asset pricing models, typically reliant on linear relationships, miss.

In addition to asset return predictions, the estimation of co-movements between asset returns plays an important role when constructing portfolios. These co-movements are usually described in a covariance matrix. Estimating well-conditioned, stable covariance matrices poses significant challenges, as it requires extensive historical time series data, especially as the number of assets increases and dependency structures become more complex. The estimation risk increases even further if the number of assets is in the same order of magnitude as the number of observations, the so-called "curse of dimensionality". However, MVO requires stable covariance matrices to function effectively. ML methods can help create such covariance matrices, for example by using hierarchical clustering; an unsupervised learning method for clustering data points, as demonstrated by the hierarchical risk parity (HRP) approach (López de Prado, 2016). By clustering similar assets, less parameters need to be estimated. HRP then constructs a diversified portfolio based on the information in the covariance matrix. The resulting portfolios tend to be more diversified and less concentrated compared to the ones constructed based on MVO. Further advancements of the HRP method aim to make it more adaptable, accurate, and robust (Raffinot, 2018).

9.2.2 *Advanced AI Optimization Techniques*

In the literature, two AI approaches have emerged as particularly prominent for portfolio optimization: deep reinforcement learning (DRL) and evolutionary algorithms (EA). The study by Benhamou et al. (2020) applies DRL to continuously adjust portfolio weights by interacting with the market environment and adapting to changing market conditions. Thus, the focus is on adaptive strategies rather than predictive models as in supervised learning. The empirical results demonstrate that their DRL model outperformed traditional portfolio optimization methods. On the other hand, the study of Branke et al. (2009) employs EA that mimic an evolutionary process in order to find an optimal solution. This approach is computationally more efficient than traditional methods and thus can be applied to more complex asset allocation problems, such as problems with cardinality constraints (if the number of assets in a portfolio is limited). It is primarily used to solve static portfolio optimization problems, in contrast to DRL methods, which are more suitable for dynamic optimization problems.

These are empirical findings, and more research is needed to determine whether AI consistently offers better estimates of risk and return and superior portfolio optimization methods than traditional methods, given the problem- and data-dependent nature of current studies. However, the results suggest, that already today AI can be efficiently used to help Portfolio Managers assess and refine their current positioning.

9.2.3 *Integrating Sustainability Goals into Portfolio Optimization*

Extending these AI based portfolio optimization approaches to incorporate sustainability goals, which could even be client-specific, requires further research. Such goals may be included via constraints, e.g. by over (under) weighting sectors or companies that perform well (poor) according to certain sustainability characteristics. Furthermore, portfolio optimization allows managers to pursue specific sustainability ratings or environmental objectives, such as carbon emissions reduction, while effectively managing the portfolio's tracking error. Tracking error, refers to the deviation of a portfolio's returns from its benchmark, reflecting the level of risk taken by the manager to outperform the benchmark. Portfolio managers can align sustainability goals with performance objectives, ensuring that deviations from the benchmark remain within predefined limits. However, portfolio managers must be aware of the inherent challenges associated with ESG (Environmental, Social, Governance) datasets and methodologies (Kirby et al., 2021). These challenges include limited historical data, issues with comparability across metrics, and gaps in coverage, particularly within certain asset classes and geographic regions.

9.2.4 Large Language Models in Portfolio Management

With the rise of LLMs in recent years, new use cases of AI within portfolio management have emerged. One use case is investment analysis that can be significantly enhanced and made more efficient, using LLMs as well as traditional natural language processing (NLP) techniques. Since one of the key advantages of LLMs is their ability to process and summarize large amounts of unstructured text data, they are highly relevant for investment and company analysis, as these tasks are performed mostly manually in today's financial industry. Text data, that is usually being analyzed, when deciding whether to invest in the stock of a given public company or not, are news articles, company filings, financial statements, and social media posts. One example uses ChatGPT-4 for financial statement analysis (Foy, 2023). Another application is BloombergGPT, which is claimed to be the first large language model for the financial domain, reported in literature. This 50-billion parameter language model is trained on both financial datasets as well as general datasets (Wu et al., 2023). Use-cases of BloombergGPT range from financial sentiment analysis, document summarization (e.g. financial statements), market trend predictions to data extraction and customer support resulting in improved decision-making, efficiency and automation within the financial industry.

Further, LLMs can be used for sentiment analysis. Sentiment analysis gauges market sentiment towards specific companies or assets and thus could inform investment decisions. In addition, analyzing a vast amount of news and social media surrounding a specific company can be useful in identifying potential risks and opportunities, including those related to sustainability factors. One example of applying sentiment analysis to corporate annual reports is the DL based approach from Azimi and Agrawal (2021). The authors discover that positive and negative sentiments play a key role in predicting abnormal returns around the 10-K filing date, as well as future company fundamentals and policies. This finding indicates that the qualitative information in corporate annual reports is more insightful than previously recognized. However, the practical applicability of such approaches in real-world investment processes still needs to be further assessed.

Future potential applications for LLMs could be in the field of sustainable investment analysis. Such applications could enhance the sustainability assessment of companies as well as the assessment of transition risks. Hereby, using public data on a given company, such as company news, social media or sustainability reports, and enhancing it with proprietary sustainability metrics (ratings, etc.) to help answer questions such as how credible a company's transition plan is more efficiently.

Another potential application is the creation of synthetic market scenarios that replicate the statistical properties of real market data. This approach can enhance traditional stress testing and scenario analysis methods, helping portfolio managers testing and optimizing their investment strategies, resp. gaining a deeper understanding of how a given strategy performs in various market scenarios. The implementation of such applications can be realized through a technology called "retrieval-augmented generation" (RAG) (Lewis et al., 2020). Hereby, LLMs are combined with external data sources, e.g. databases or the web, in order to build LLM-powered applications with improved accuracy and relevant information. One real world example applies this technology directly to the area of portfolio optimization (Radovanovic, 2023) with the use of AutoGPT. AutoGPT, built on GPT-4, can pursue a user-specified goal by creating a plan and formulating tasks, that it then executes with minimal human intervention. Such models are also called "AI agents". Potential general steps in an LLM-powered application using RAG are gathering data from various sources (public as well as company internal or client data), perform calculations and finally generating reports and summaries.

While AI shows significant potential to transform areas such as (sustainable) investment analysis and portfolio management, further research is still needed, and we are only at the beginning of understanding its full impact and capabilities.

9.3 Leveraging Artificial Intelligence and Machine Learning for Climate Risk and Fraud Detection in Wealth Management

The financial services industry is increasingly starting to adopt AI and ML approaches within their risk management departments, such as in credit risk, e.g. in the evaluation of loan applications, as well as market risk when predicting market shifts. However, in this subchapter we would like to focus on applications within climate risk as well as operational risk.

The financial risks associated with climate change are significant, thereby impacting also the wealth management industry. Such risks can be divided into physical risk and transition risk. Physical risk is financial loss due to physical damages of property and infrastructure from increasingly frequent and severe extreme weather events - annual losses for global insurers are forecasted to be USD 151bn (Matthewson, 2024). Transition risk, on the other hand, arises from the financial and social impacts associated with adapting to a lower-carbon economy.

The financial system's focus on short-term performance further neglects the long-term effects of climate change, needed for a truly sustainable investment approach. ML methods can help mitigate these financial risks, as has been investigated by the Association for Computing Machinery (ACM). For example, climate analytics uses predictive approaches to address climate change by forecasting the financial effects of climate change (Rolnick et al., 2022). It can be utilized to identify climate risks as well as investment opportunities by employing NLP to analyze company disclosures, news articles and other data sources. Further climate analytics entails the assessment of investment portfolios in order to identify climate risk exposures using ML methods. In addition, the prediction of carbon prices in emissions trading schemes can be tackled with ML methods. This helps investors to better manage their exposure to carbon risk. By using these techniques, investment portfolios can be steered to be more climate resilient, e.g. by the construction of carbon neutral portfolios that focus on companies with low carbon emissions or by employing best-in-class portfolios, which select top-performing companies within each sector based on sustainability and climate-related criteria. ML methods can also help to create "green" indices towards which investment portfolios can be managed. Future research and practice will help reveal how climate analytics can be used to better measure and manage climate-related financial risks.

In the wealth management industry, fraud detection — a critical component of operational risk management — has become increasingly important in the age of AI, as fraud schemes grow more sophisticated at exploiting new vulnerabilities. Hence, firms must continuously enhance their risk and control frameworks to stay ahead of these evolving threats. Since traditional methods for fraud detection are often based on rules, defined by humans, they are unable to detect more complex fraud schemes. Another challenge with traditional, often too coarse, methods poses their too high false positive rate, meaning the system flags potential fraud that later proves to be a false alarm. This results in additional costs for the company trying to distinguish false alerts from real ones (van Liebergen, 2017). AI and ML methods are better at identifying complex patterns in vast amounts of data, e.g. transaction data, be it patterns based on historical data but also identifying emerging patterns in new data. According to Ngai et al. (2011), the two most important AI methods used in financial fraud detection are neural networks as well as decision trees. Typical areas where AI approaches are employed involve transaction monitoring, to detect money laundering as well as finding connections between clients in order to assess their riskiness. An increasing number of companies and start-ups are offering their services in this area to financial institutions. One example is Feedzai (n.d.), which specializes in using AI for fraud detection. Feedzai's platform is widely used, e.g. Lloyds Banking and Citibank.

9.4 AI-Underpinnned Personalized Wealth Management

A survey by Accenture (2022) showed that more than eight out of 10 financial advisors believe that AI's greatest benefit is translating the clients' data into actionable insight for their benefit. Looking at the literature, it can be confirmed that AI can play an important role in enhancing the client experience along customer acquisition, onboarding and retention.

In the context of **customer acquisition**, AI can be helpful for customer segmentation, content creation, and distribution.

Beyond the traditional **customer segmentation** methods, AI can analyze large datasets to identify patterns, enabling the creation of more granular or "micro-segmentation" of customers. This process can occur in real-time and may include predictive modeling for future user behaviors (Mitolo, 2023).

Additionally, LLMs can **generate content** and images for marketing and sales by leveraging existing examples and data, thereby enhancing productivity (Deng, et al., 2024). In some cases, users found the AI-created content more appealing than the human-made, and that it can significantly improve customer brand experience and attachment (Rix et al., 2022, Tran et al., 2023). The underlying technology for these use cases usually combines Application Programming Interfaces (APIs) and back-end databases (Deng, et al., 2024). J.P. Morgan Research (2023) thinks that GenAI could revolutionize content creation across text, code, images, video, 3D and gaming, likely reaching its full potential in 2030.

Equipped with that knowledge, content can be planned and **distributed** in a very targeted manner in terms of timing, medium, and channel, aiming for higher campaign effectiveness (Arun Kumar, 2021). Beheshti et al. (2020) coin the term cognitive recommender system; a system that goes beyond the traditional recommender system by using explicit and implicit behavioural patterns to build a user's personality graph as the underlying logic to distribute highly targeted content. Explicit patterns include demographics, location history and text shared online, such as posts or reviews. Implicit behavioral patterns can be categorized into methods that analyze social features, trust, and actions to make recommendations. They include for instance the detection of a person's personality type through AI. Personalized follow-up messages and the distribution of highly relevant content according to the user's "propensity to buy" at the preferred time of the day of device interaction represent another lever for AI to increase marketing and sales effectiveness potentially.

Chatbots support the prospect and client throughout the customer lifecycle. The Future Today Institute (2017) defines a bot as an AI-enabled software application to automate specific tasks. With 24/7 availability, they can become an important sparring partner to the relationship managers for client services, portfolio analysis, and educational purposes. Wells Fargo for instance employs Chatbot Erika across web and mobile application to help clients with basic transactions and account queries around the clock (Deng et al. 2024, Jain, 2023).

Based on a client's baseline financial literacy, chatbots can customize educational content to help clients deepen their financial knowledge. On top of that, by analyzing previous client interactions, the tone, style, and frequency of chatbot services can be adapted to fit the clients' preferences, another lever to increase customer experience and loyalty (Ramjattan et al., 2021).

During **customer onboarding and retention**, AI-technology can add further value.

AI can for instance enhance the effectiveness and customer satisfaction of the **financial planning process**. By enabling more detailed client risk profiling than traditional methods, AI provides a deeper understanding of client behavior and preferences. This improvement is not only due to the increased availability and processing of data but also because clients and their advisors can explore relevant simulations and scenarios together that would feel more real to the client. These tools allow for a clearer view of client behavior and preferences than traditional approaches (Financial Times & Standard Chartered, 2024).

Goal-based financial planning enabled by AI can help cater to clients' needs across their lifetimes. Similar to human financial advisors, the system takes a holistic approach to changing saving objectives across a lifetime, assets, risk profile, cash flow, economic conditions, historical performance, and personal preferences. Therewith, the system can standalone for retail or as a support tool for client advisors, cater to multiple objectives for savings and investment with the help of Large Language Models (LLMs) and reinforcement learning. Vanguard operates a tool that follows this thought process (Mohammed et al., 2021).

In recent literature, AI-enabled budget optimization has also become a topic of democratizing financial planning. AI-agents supporting individuals or households to optimize for the income vs spending ratio with the support of LLMs can be very effective (De Zarzà et al., 2023). The same counts for debt and tax management systems. Such solutions could therefore contribute to better personal finance management (Chak et al., 2022, Challoumis, 2024).

A digital platform that combines various of the elements above is modern-day **robo-advisory**. A robo-advisor is an algorithm-based digital platform that offers automated financial advice and/or investment management services.

The earliest robo-advisors, introduced around 1980, relied on straightforward, rule-based algorithms and systems. These tools were primarily used by investment managers, traders, and brokers to assist with portfolio management and trading decisions. Robo-advisors for end-clients have been in use for several years. One of the first notable platforms providing financial and investment advice to a wider audience with the help of rule-based algorithms was the Betterment robo-advisory platform launched in 2010. Along with other players, it disrupted traditional finance with low-cost, easily accessible, low-bias, and seamless banking and wealth management services (Ignatev, 2023; Rohner & Uhl, 2019). Evidence from Rohner and Uhl (2019) suggests, that customers can increase their annual savings potential with robo-advisors versus with traditional investment advice.

Today's robo-advisors can incorporate goal-based financial planning, wealth management, chatbots and advertise their services more effectively with AI-underpinned solutions. Powered by natural language processing (NLP) and machine learning algorithms, the combination of those tools is powerful enough to provide a personalized, conversational, and natural experience for clients.

Yet, availability doesn't equal adoption. Qualitative results suggest that customer satisfaction is highest when robo-advisory service is coupled with human interaction regarding key robo-advisory features such as investor profiling, investment strategy and evaluation (Barile et al., 2024). A paper from Piotrowski & Orzeszko (2023) suggests, that consumers' willingness to use robo-advisory is strongly dependent on their trust in the financial institution offering it, and less so on the general openness of the consumer to technology. Another study focused on millennials (Yi et al., 2023) found that financial savviness and the degree of transparency and thus trust greatly influence the willingness to use robo-advisory. One bold forecast by PwC (2023) foresees Assets under management of robo/advisors to more than double by 2027. While the trend will most likely continue for the adoption of robo-advisory services due to demographic changes of wealth owners, adoption of AI-underpinned robo advisory services is also dependent on legal frameworks, that are yet to become more robust with regards to ethical AI implementation at scale.

Given these advancements, the **role of financial advisors** may undergo a fundamental shift in the next decades that needs to be supported by a culture that fosters innovation and encourages adaptability. On the one hand, financial advisors could spend up to 65% less time on repetitive tasks and more tasks on value adding client acquisition and retention activities (Baecker et al., 2024). Advisors' true added value will increasingly stem from their ability to interpret and utilize the more nuanced financial market insights AI provides, as well as their personality, experience, perspective, and network they can bring to advise clients on their needs (Challoumis, 2024).

9.5 AI-Enhanced Operational Efficiency Within Wealth Management

In addition to enhancing core wealth management functions, AI can bring substantial efficiencies to middle and back-office operations. According to a study by Oliver Wyman, generative AI has the potential to save 25–50% of employee time in areas like operations, legal, and compliance through automation and improved process efficiency (Morgan Stanley & Oliver Wyman, 2023).

Other middle and back-office tasks—such as trade settlement, collateral management, corporate action processing, regulatory reporting, legal compliance, and system maintenance—often involve repetitive processes that are well-suited to automation technologies like robotic process automation (RPA). RPA, a rule-based technology, can perform specific tasks on a set schedule at scale. It streamlines operational processes, reduces the need for human intervention and increases accuracy and speed while reducing costs (Javaid, 2024). Also a core component of regulatory technology (RegTech), RPA plays an essential role in risk management and compliance, streamlining complex processes to help firms meet regulatory requirements more effectively (Olaiya et al., 2024).

A practical example, where AI enhances operational efficiency is deployed at JP Morgan. Their software platform called COIN, which stands for contract intelligence, leverages AI to automate the review of complex legal documents, particularly commercial loan agreements, reducing time and errors compared to manual processes. It significantly improved operational efficiency by saving 360,000 h of work annually, enabling legal teams to focus on more complex tasks (Bestpractice.ai, 2018).

Some research also looks at the fusion of AI and blockchain to reach heightened levels of security and transparency (Rane et al., 2023). However, this is beyond the scope of this chapter and readers are encouraged to explore the topic separately.

9.6 Opportunities and Challenges

The opportunities AI can unlock are manifold. From democratization of investment advice, to increasing operational efficiencies and effectiveness in client interaction with better customer insights. Yet, the very same technologies bear their own unique challenges.

First and foremost, the **black-box nature** of many AI tools can impede adoption and acceptance by practitioners, clients and regulators. When using AI-tools to i.e. determine interest rates for clients' mortgages, there is often little insight into how a machine arrived at a certain result, leaving the practitioner with doubts about acting accordingly. Clients face a similar issue, when given investment advice without knowing the logic applied. Also regulators demand high levels of transparency, which AI often cannot provide (Weber et al., 2023).

One strain of research that could provide a remedy is Explainable Artificial Intelligence (XAI). Barredo Arietta et al. (2020, p. 6) define it as follows "Given an audience, an explainable Artifcial Intelligence is one that produces details or reasons to make its functioning clear or easy to understand." It could therewith cater to the following goals: trustworthiness, causality, transferability, informativeness, confidence, fairness, accessibility, interactivity, and privacy awareness (Barredo Arietta et al., 2020). Some AI models, such as decision trees, are explainable by design and would only require a translation from technical to general language. Other AI models are black-box by nature and need "post-hoc explainability" models as add-on narrators after the fact. These post-hoc models can be specifically fitted or agnostic, depending on the architecture of the neural network. Research for "post-hoc explainability" has increased in recent years with the increase of black-box AI applications in Finance (Weber et al., 2023).

Secondly, LLMs as well as traditional NLP techniques come with problems of **content authenticity and harmful content production** that does not reflect reality. So far, no real remedy has been found. AI watermarking is an emerging technique for content verification, copyright protection, and ownership tracking. However, this watermark can currently be easily removed by simply having another LLM rephrase the watermarked content. Until recently, scalability proved problematic, too. Only a recent study has proven large-scale production systems of AI watermarking possible through a specific technique (Dathathri et al., 2024).

Hallucinations, or the fact that LLMs can produce inaccurate information, is another common problem for implementing AI in finance. Even advanced LLMs such as Chat Gpt-3.5 produced accurate output less than 25% of the time. Accuracy shrinks as generated text length increases (Guan et al., 2024). The field distinguishes between faithfulness hallucinations, where the model drifts away from instruction and factual hallucinations, where inaccurate information is provided. The sources of hallucinations in LLM development include flawed data sources, data handling, training or inference design flaws (Huang et al., 2025).

A paper by Duang et al. (2024) found empirical evidence that LLMs have some awareness of their hallucinations. This seems to be particularly true for smaller models, those without instruction finetuning, and those who have access to external knowledge (RAG).

Whereby instructional fine-tuning in AI describes the process of adjusting a model's training using specific, task-focused instructions to increase its ability to follow commands and produce desired responses.

Also, prompts boosting the model's confidence have been seen to increase their hallucination awareness. Yet, more research needs to confirm these first findings. According to Guan et al. (2024), LLM-based fact verifiers can prove effective in verifying LLM output. More evidence is needed to see if this type of fact verification can be applicable in real-world scenarios at scale.

Another challenge to be addressed with AI in finance are **Biases**. Research distinguishes different sources of AI bias. Data biases come in the form of underrepresentation in the original data set and/or during training on non-representative data. The second relates to the design of the AI system itself, whereby the model could incorrectly derive certain generalizations from correlations, i.e. exclude certain socioeconomic groups by default (Varsha, 2023). Dealing with AI flaws is critical, as they can have multiple impacts on fundamental human rights, social and economic discrimination, as well as negatively impact the business of those using flawed AI systems (Bansal et al., 2023). XAI, improved data quality and diversity, regulations and collaboration can work against such biases, but are only as effective as the creators and users want them to be.

From a **legal perspective**, several actors are important on a European level for the implementation of AI without data bias. The European AI Office is the expertise center for AI across the European Union and a key player in implementing the AI act. The European AI Act aims to "address risks to health, safety and fundamental rights" and is directed to all public and private actors in the European Union. It clusters AI-systems in different risk categories and provides respective obligations (European Comission, 2024).

Additionally, the European Financial Data Space (EFDS) aims to create a more inclusive financial market by promoting data sharing mainly among financial institutions. It can help increase the data pool available to AI training and reduce reliance on biased historical data. However, EFDS only relies on customer consent for data sharing, excludes third-party providers that do not qualify as financial institutions, and does not share information on creditworthiness. EFDS is subject to the General Data Protection Regulation (GDPR).

The GDPR provides legal boundaries for the collection, storage and processing of personal data. It therewith is of utmost importance for responsible AI development from a consumer perspective. In its broad terms, it makes consumer consent necessary for utilizing personalized data and determines that existing data sets need to be anonymized before utilizing AI. Yet, anonymization requirements under

GDPR are rather weak, and re-identification to the individual could be possible Also, the use of anonymized data makes specific AI methods, i.e. NLP, to date impossible to be completed successfully at scale (Gruschka et al., 2018).

9.7 Conclusion and Outlook

AI has emerged as a transformative force in wealth management. By leveraging advanced technologies like machine learning, deep learning, and generative AI, wealth managers can address evolving client needs, optimize portfolios, and improve decision-making processes. However, these opportunities are accompanied with challenges related to sustainability in the wider sense, such as transparency, ethical considerations, and data governance that need to be solved to adopt AI in ever more delicate domains at scale. Very likely, AI will continue to become a cornerstone for the industry's evolution.

References

Accenture. (2022). AI in wealth management. https://www.accenture.com/content/dam/accenture/final/a-com-migration/r3-3/pdf/pdf-178/accenture-wealth-management-ai-all-systems-go.pdf#zoom=40.

Arun Kumar, B. R. (2021). AI-based digital marketing strategies—a review. Lecture Notes in Networks and Systems. https://doi.org/10.1007/978-981-33-4305-4_70.

Azimi, M., & Agrawal, A. (2021). Is positive sentiment in corporate annual reports informative? Evidence from deep learning. *The Review of Asset Pricing Studies, 11*(4), 762–805.

Baecker, P., Helbing, C., Shah, R., Descamps, G., & Mehta, B. (2024, March 11). How bank CIOs can build a solid foundation for generative AI. Bain. https://www.bain.com/insights/how-bank-cios-can-build-a-solid-foundation-for-generative-ai.

Bansal, C., Pandey, K., Goel, R., Sharma, A., & Jangirala, S. (2023). Artificial intelligence (AI) bias impacts: Classification framework for effective mitigation. *Issues in Information Systems, 24*(4), 367–389. https://doi.org/10.48009/4_iis_2023_128

Barile, D., Secundo, G., & Bussoli, C. (2024, April 25). Exploring artificial intelligence robo-advisor in banking industry: A platform model. Management Decision, Vol. ahead-of-print No. ahead-of-print. https://doi.org/10.1108/MD-08-2023-1324.

Barredo Arrieta, A., Díaz-Rodríguez, N., Del Ser, J., Bennetot, A., Tabik, S., Barbado, A., Garcia, S., Gil-Lopez, S., Molina, D., Benjamins, R., Chatila, R., & Herrera, F. (2020). Explainable artificial intelligence (XAI): Concepts, taxonomies, opportunities and challenges toward responsible AI. *Information Fusion, 58*, 82–115. https://doi.org/10.1016/j.inffus.2019.12.012

Beheshti, A., Yakhchi, S., Mousaeirad, S., Ghafari, S. M., Goluguri, S. R., & Edrisi, M. A. (2020, July 22). *Towards cognitive recommender systems*. Department of Computing, Macquarie University, Macquarie Park 2109, Australia. https://www.mdpi.com/1999-4893/13/8/176.

Benhamou, E., Saltiel, D., Ohana, J. J., Atif, J., & Laraki, R. (2020). Deep reinforcement learning (DRL) for portfolio allocation. *ECML PKDD 2020 workshops*. (pp. 527–531).

Bestpractice.ai. (2018). *JPMorgan reduced lawyers' hours by 36...—AI case study JPMorgan.* https://www.bestpractice.ai/studies/jpmorgan_reduced_lawyers_hours_by_360_000_annually_by_automating_loan_agreement_analysis_with_machine_learning_software_coin.

Branke, J., Scheckenbach, B., Stein, M., Deb, K., & Schmeck, H. (2009). Portfolio optimization with an envelope-based multi-objective evolutionary algorithm. *European Journal of Operational Research, 199*(3), 684–693.

Caserta, J., Harreis, H., Rowshankish, K., Srinidhi, N., & Tavakoli, A. (2023). The data dividend: Fueling generative AI. McKinsey & Company. Retrieved November 26, 2024, from https://www.mckinsey.com/~/media/mckinsey/business%20functions/mckinsey%20digital/our%20insights/the%20data%20dividend%20fueling%20generative%20ai/the-data-dividend-fueling-generative-ai.pdf.

Chak, I., Croxson, K., D'Acunto, F., Reuter, J., Rossi, A. G., & Shaw, J. M. (2022, November). *Improving household debt management with Robo-advice*. National Bureau of Economic Research | NBER. https://www.nber.org/system/files/working_papers/w30616/w30616.pdf.

Challoumis, C. (2024, October 3). AI in wealth management - transforming personal finance for the better. XVI international scientific conference. Philadelphia. USA. https://conference-w.com/wp-content/uploads/2024/10/USA.P-0304102024.pdf#page=31.

Cortes, C., & Vapnik, V. (1995). A training algorithm for optimal margin classifiers. *Proceedings of the 5th annual ACM workshop on computational learning theory*. (pp. 273–297).

Dathathri, S., See, A., Ghaisas, S., et al. (2024). Scalable watermarking for identifying large language model outputs. *Nature, 634*, 818–823. https://doi.org/10.1038/s41586-024-08025-4

Deng, T., Bi, S., Wang, J., Xiao, J., & Bao, W. (2024). Customer-centric AI in banking: Using AIGC to improve personalized services. *Journal of Artificial Intelligence Practice*. Clausius Scientific Press, Canada. https://www.clausiuspress.com/assets/default/article/2024/07/22/article_1721655632.pdf

De Zarzà, I., De Curtò, J., Roig, G., & Calafate, C. T. (2023, December 25). Optimized financial planning: Integrating individual and cooperative budgeting models with LLM recommendations. *AI 2024, 5*(1), 91–114. https://doi.org/10.3390/ai5010006

Duang, H., Yang, Y., & Tam, K. Y. (2024). Do LLMs know about hallucination? An Empirical Investigation of LLM's Hidden States. Department of Information Systems, Business Statistics and Operations Management, The Hong Kong University of Science and Technology. https://arxiv.org/pdf/2402.09733.

European Comission. (2024, August 1). *Artificial intelligence—questions and answers*. https://ec.europa.eu/commission/presscorner/detail/en/qanda_21_1683.

Feedzai. (n.d.). Retrieved November 26, 2024, from https://www.feedzai.com/.

Financial Times & Standard Chartered. (2024). AI and the dawn of hyper-personalisation in wealth management. https://www.ft.com/partnercontent/standard-chartered/ai-and-the-dawn-of-hyper-personalisation-in-wealth-management.html.

Foy, P. (2023). GPT-4 for financial statements: Building an AI analyst. MLQ.ai. Retrieved November 26, 2024, from https://blog.mlq.ai/gpt-4-financial-statements-ai-analyst/.

Gruschka, N., Mavroeidis, V., Vishi, K., & Jensen, M. (2018). Privacy issues and data protection in big data: A case study analysis under GDPR. In *2018 IEEE international conference on big data (big data)* (pp. 5027–5033). https://doi.org/10.1109/BigData.2018.8622621

Gu, S., Kelly, B., & Xiu, D. (2020). Empirical asset pricing via machine learning. *The Review of Financial Studies, 33*(5), 2223–2273. https://doi.org/10.1093/rfs/hhaa009

Guan, J., Dodge, J., Wadden, D., Huang, M., & Peng, H. (2024). *Language models hallucinate, but may Excel at fact verification*. https://doi.org/10.48550/arXiv.2310.14564. https://arxiv.org/abs/2310.14564.

Haykin, S. (1999). *Neural networks: A comprehensive foundation*. Pearson.

Huang, L., Yu, W., Ma, W., Zhong, W., Feng, Z., Wang, H., Chen, Q., Peng, W., Feng, X., Qin, B., & Liu, T. (2025). A survey on hallucination in large language models: Principles, taxonomy, challenges, and open questions. *ACM Transactions on Information Systems, 43*(2) Art. No.: 42, 1–55. https://doi.org/10.1145/370315

Ignatev, M. (2023). The evolution and implications of Robo-advisors and their impact on traditional financial institutions. LAB University of Applied Sciences. https://www.theseus.fi/bitstream/handle/10024/816836/Ignatev_Mikhail.pdf?sequence=2.

Isaacson, W. (2014). *The innovators: How a group of hackers, geniuses, and geeks created the digital revolution*. Simon & Schuster.
Jain, R. (2023). Role of artificial intelligence in banking and finance. *Journal of Management and Science, 13*(3), 1–4. https://jmseleyon.com/index.php/jms/article/view/678/652
Javaid, H. A. (2024). The future of financial services: Integrating AI for smarter, more efficient operations. *MZ Journal of Artificial Intelligence, 1*(2) https://mzjournal.com/index.php/MZJAI/article/view/239/237
J.P. Morgan Research. (2023, March 20). The rise of generative AI. J.P. Morgan | Official Website. https://www.jpmorgan.com/insights/global-research/artificial-intelligence/generative-ai.
Kirby, A., Lofts, G., & Tattersall, P. (2021, July 5). Why data remains the biggest ESG investing challenge for asset managers. Ernst & Young Global Limited. Retrieved November 26, 2024, from https://www.ey.com/en_gl/insights/financial-services/emeia/why-data-remains-the-biggest-esg-investing-challenge-for-asset-managers?
Lewis, P., Perez, E., Piktus, A., Petroni, F., Karpukhin, V., Goyal, N., et al. (2020). Retrieval-augmented generation for knowledge-intensive nlp tasks. *Advances in Neural Information Processing Systems, 33*, 9459–9474.
Lloyd, S. P. (1982). Least squares quantization in PCM. *IEEE Transactions on Information Theory, 28*(2), 129–137. https://doi.org/10.1109/TIT.1982.1056489
López de Prado, M. (2016). Building diversified portfolios that outperform out-of-sample. *Journal of Portfolio Management, 42*(4), 59–69.
Mitolo, A. L. (2023). Unveiling novel AI use-cases in marketing: Bridging the gap between AI innovations and marketing core processes for effective communication with marketing professionals. Repository University of Twente Student Theses. https://essay.utwente.nl/95322/1/Mitolo_BA_BMS.pdf.
Morgan, S., & Oliver, W. (2023). The AI tipping point. Bluepaper. https://www.oliverwyman.com/content/dam/oliver-wyman/v2/publications/2023/october/Oliver_Wyman_Morgan_Stanley_Global_Wealth_and_Asset_Management_report_2023_The_Generative_AI_Tipping%20Point1.pdf.
Olaiya, O. P., Adesoga, T. O., Pieterson, K., Obani, O. Q., Adebayo, J. O., & Ajayi, O. O. (2024). *RegTech solutions: Enhancing compliance and risk management in the financial industry*. Global Scholarly Communication Online Press | International Online Open Access Publisher. https://doi.org/10.30574/gscarr.2024.20.2.0295
PricewaterhouseCoopers. (2023). AI and wealth management: A new era. PwC. https://www.pwc.com/gx/en/issues/c-suite-insights/the-leadership-agenda/ai-and-wealth-management-a-new-era.html.
Piotrowski, D., & Orzeszko, W. (2023). Artificial intelligence and customers' intention to use robo-advisory in banking services. *Equilibrium. Quarterly Journal of Economics and Economic Policy, 18*(4), 967–1007. https://doi.org/10.24136/eq.2023.031
Raffinot, T. (2018). The hierarchical equal risk contribution portfolio. *SSRN Electronic Journal*. https://doi.org/10.2139/ssrn.3237540
Ramjattan, R., Hosein, P., & Henry, N. (2021). Using chatbot technologies to help individuals make sound personalized financial decisions. *IEEE International Humanitarian Technology Conference (IHTC)*. https://doi.org/10.1109/IHTC53077.2021.9698928
Rohner, P., & Uhl, M. (2019). Robo-advisors vs. traditional investment advisors—an unequal game. *Journal of Wealth Management, Summer 2018, 21*(1), 44–50. https://doi.org/10.3905/jwm.2018.21.1.044
Rolnick, D., Donti, P. L., Kaack, L. H., Kochanski, K., Lacoste, A., Sankaran, K., et al. (2022). Tackling climate change with machine learning. *ACM Computing Surveys (CSUR), 55*(2), 1–96.
Markowitz, H. (1952). Portfolio selection. *The Journal of Finance, 7*(1), 77–91. https://doi.org/10.2307/2975974
Matthewson, A. (2024, September 5). Verisk 2024 global modeled catastrophe losses. InsurTech Digital. Retrieved on November 26, 2024, from https://insurtechdigital.com/articles/verisk-2024-global-modelled-catastrophe-losses.

Ngai, E. W. T., Hu, Y. H., Wong, Y. H., Chen, Y., & Sun, X. (2011). The application of data mining techniques in financial fraud detection: A classification framework and an academic review of literature. *Decision Support Systems, 50*(3), 559–569.
Quinlan, J. R. (1986). Induction of decision trees. *Machine Learning, 1*(1), 81–106.
Radovanovic, I. (2023, May). Auto-GPT for finance—an exploratory guide. AlgoTrading101. Retrieved on November 26, 2024, from https://algotrading101.com/learn/auto-gpt-finance-guide/.
Rane, N., Choudhary, S., & Rane, J. (2023, December). *Blockchain and artificial intelligence (AI) integration for revolutionizing security and transparency in finance*. https://doi.org/10.2139/ssrn.4644253
Rix, J., Rußell, R., Rühr, A., & Hess, T. (2022). Human vs. AI: Investigating consumers' context-dependent purchase intentions for algorithm-created content. https://scholarspace.manoa.hawaii.edu/items/b8cf91b4-602e-43e1-b293-23031ac47c20.
Rojas, R. (1996). Perceptron learning. In *Neural networks: A systematic introduction* (pp. 77–98). Springer.
Russell, S. J., & Norvig, P. (2021). *Artificial intelligence: A modern approach* (4th ed.). Pearson.
The Future Today Institute. (2017). Tech Trends. https://futuretodayinstitute.com/2017-tech-trends.
Mohammed, S., Bealer, R., & Cohen, J. (2021). *Embracing advanced AI/ML to help investors achieve success: Vanguard's reinforcement learning for financial goal planning*. The Vanguard Group, Inc. https://arxiv.org/pdf/2110.12003
Tran, T., Sen, S., & Steenburg, E. V. (2023). This ad's for you: How personalized SNS advertisements affect the consumer–brand relationship. *Journal of Consumer Marketing*.. https://www.emerald.com. https://doi.org/10.1108/jcm-12-2021-5070/full/html
Turing, A. M. (1950). Computing machinery and intelligence. *Mind, 59*(236), 433–460. https://doi.org/10.1093/mind/LIX.236.433
van Liebergen, B. (2017). *Machine learning in compliance risk management*. Institute of International Finance.
Varsha, P. S. (2023). How can we manage biases in artificial intelligence systems—a systematic literature review. School of Commerce, Presidency University, Bangalore, India. https://doi.org/10.1016/j.jjimei.2023.100165
Vaswani, A., Shazeer, N., Parmar, N., Uszkoreit, J., Jones, L., Gomez, A. N., Kaiser, Ł., & Polosukhin, I. (2017). Attention is all you need. *Advances in Neural Information Processing Systems, 30*. https://doi.org/10.48550/arXiv.1706.03762
Weber, P., Carl, K. V., & Hinz, O. (2023). Applications of explainable artificial intelligence in finance—a systematic review of finance, information systems, and computer science literature. *Management Review Quartlery*. https://doi.org/10.1007/s11301-023-00320-0
Wu, S., İrsoy, O., Lu, S., Dabravolski, V., Dredze, M., Gehrmann, S., ... & Mann, G. (2023). BloombergGPT: A large language model for finance. *arXiv preprint arXiv:2303.17564*.
Yi, T. Z., Rom, N. A. M., Hassan, N. M., Samsurijan, M. S., & Ebekozien, A. (2023). The adoption of Robo-advisory among millennials in the 21st century: Trust, usability and knowledge perception. *Sustainability, 15*(7), 6016. https://doi.org/10.3390/su15076016

Chapter 10
Learn or Loose: Wealth Management Needs Female Wealth Managers

Karen Wendt and Marta Ra

10.1 Introduction: The Importance of Female Wealth Managers

The wealth management industry has traditionally been male-dominated, with women often underrepresented both in client advisory roles and in decision-making positions. However, in recent years, the role of female wealth managers has become increasingly important, not only in diversifying perspectives but also in driving new trends in investment strategies and client relationship management. The growth of female wealth managers is a key response to the evolving needs of female investors, who often have different priorities and risk profiles compared to their male counterparts.

Case Study A notable example is the rise of Sallie Krawcheck, the CEO of Ellevest, a digital wealth management platform designed specifically for women. Krawcheck, a former Wall Street executive, identified the gaps in the wealth management industry where female investors were underserved. Ellevest's platform focuses on investment strategies that cater to women's financial needs, including their longer lifespans and career interruptions due to caregiving. Krawcheck's business model has been praised for addressing women's unique financial needs and challenges (Ellevest, 2021).

K. Wendt
President Sustainable Finance, Eccos Impact GmbH, Cham, Switzerland
e-mail: karen@sustainablefinance.io

M. Ra (✉)
Women In Sustainable Finance (WISF), Zurich, Switzerland
e-mail: marta.ra@wisfinternational.com

K. Wendt, M. Ra (eds.), *Sustainable Wealth Management Revisited*, Sustainable Finance, https://doi.org/10.1007/978-3-032-02530-2_10

10.2 The Rise of Female Wealth Managers

Historically, the wealth management sector has been heavily skewed towards male professionals. However, the presence of female wealth managers has steadily increased as firms recognize the value of gender diversity in financial advisory roles. Research suggests that women tend to approach wealth management with a greater emphasis on risk management, long-term growth, and ethical investment practices. They often prioritize a more holistic view of wealth—one that considers not only financial gain but also social and environmental factors.

In the U.S., women are expected to control more than $30 trillion of wealth by 2030, which is about half of the country's wealth (Bishop, 2021). This shift has prompted a demand for wealth management services tailored to the values and needs of female investors. As more women ascend to executive roles within wealth management firms, they bring new insights that help shape a more inclusive approach to financial planning.

10.3 Women's Investment Preferences and Risk Management

10.3.1 Risk Management for Women

One of the defining characteristics of female investors is their approach to risk. Research has shown that women are generally more risk-averse than men, particularly when it comes to investments (Kozlowski, 2001). Women's risk management style tends to be more cautious, with a preference for stable and predictable returns rather than high-risk, high-reward ventures. This risk-averse tendency is often shaped by social factors, as women have historically been more likely to take on caregiving roles and thus may prioritize financial stability to protect family wealth.

Case Study Research by Vanguard (2020) supports this, showing that women are more likely to engage in low-risk investment strategies such as bonds, compared to their male counterparts, who are typically more inclined to invest in equities. The study found that while women's portfolios were more conservative, they tended to have more stable and consistent long-term growth.

10.3.2 Value-Driven Investing

Value-driven investing is an approach that aligns investments with a person's ethical values and social priorities. Women, especially millennial and Gen Z investors, are increasingly drawn to sustainable and socially responsible investment options. This form of investing focuses on companies that demonstrate strong environmental, social, and governance (ESG) practices. In fact, studies suggest that women are more likely to incorporate ESG criteria into their investment decisions than men (Morningstar, 2019). Female wealth managers can leverage this growing trend by offering clients the opportunity to invest in a way that aligns with their values, whether it's supporting clean energy, social justice, or sustainable agriculture.

Case Study A prominent case in value-driven investing is the rise of *Sustainable Wealth* led by female financial advisors like Clara J. Wicks, who has worked to shape a new era of responsible investment. Her advisory firm, which caters specifically to women investors, emphasizes a blend of financial growth and social good, focusing on ESG investments. Wicks' approach emphasizes that women not only want financial returns but also want their investments to align with their values (Wicks, 2020).

10.4 Why Women Invest in Impact

10.4.1 The Role of Gender in Impact Investing

Impact investing, which refers to investments made with the intention to generate positive social or environmental impact alongside a financial return, has seen significant growth over the past decade. Women, particularly in the millennial and Gen Z cohorts, are leading the charge in impact investing, with a strong preference for investments that align with their personal and societal values. According to a 2020 study by the Global Impact Investing Network (GIIN), 74% of female investors consider social impact a core objective when making investments, compared to just 55% of men (GIIN, 2020).

Case Study One leading example of this trend is the *Women's Impact Fund*, which focuses on financing businesses led by women or businesses that prioritize women's rights and social empowerment. This initiative has been successful in attracting female investors who prioritize making a tangible difference in society, such as supporting women-owned businesses or advancing social justice (Women's Impact Fund, 2020).

10.4.2 Studies and Research on Female Investment Behavior

Research indicates that female investors often prefer to allocate funds towards initiatives that address systemic issues, such as climate change, poverty, and inequality (Deloitte, 2017). Studies have shown that women are more likely to invest in companies that prioritize sustainability and social responsibility, as opposed to those focused purely on financial returns (Henriksson et al., 2018). This preference is not only a reflection of personal values but also a strategic investment approach that seeks to mitigate long-term risks associated with environmental degradation and social inequality.

10.5 Women as Family and Planet-Focused Investors

10.5.1 Investing Beyond Personal Wealth

Women are increasingly recognizing their role as stewards of family wealth, making decisions that impact future generations. This is especially true for women who inherit or manage family wealth, where there is often a heightened sense of responsibility to preserve and grow the assets for their children and grandchildren. Female wealth managers are instrumental in guiding these clients toward sustainable and multi-generational financial planning.

Case Study The *Glenmede Trust* offers a strong example of wealth management that incorporates family legacy planning, and it has been especially popular among female clients. The firm provides strategies that ensure the preservation of family wealth for future generations, combining financial planning with charitable giving. Women in these families are deeply involved in managing wealth transitions, not just from a financial perspective but also in ensuring their family's values are passed down (Glenmede, 2020).

10.5.2 Influence on Family and Generational Wealth

A significant trend among female investors is the desire to involve their families in the investment process. Women tend to view financial planning not only as a tool for personal wealth accumulation but also as a way to secure a better future for their children and communities. This is evident in the increasing interest in legacy planning, which includes the integration of values-based investing into the wealth transfer process. A 2021 study by the Transamerica Center for Retirement Studies found that women are more likely to discuss financial matters with family members and pass down wealth with an emphasis on social values (Transamerica, 2021).

10.6 Creating More Opportunities for Female Wealth Managers

10.6.1 Barriers for Women in Wealth Management

Despite the growing importance of female wealth managers, significant barriers remain in terms of access to leadership positions in the wealth management industry. A 2020 study by McKinsey & Company found that women hold only 22% of senior positions in the global wealth management sector, and their representation in executive roles remains disproportionately low (McKinsey & Company, 2020). This lack of representation at the top levels of the industry limits the opportunities for female wealth managers to influence industry trends and decisions.

10.6.2 Structural and Cultural Changes Needed

To address these disparities, financial institutions must actively implement policies that promote diversity and inclusion, such as mentorship programs, leadership development, and equitable access to high-profile clients. Additionally, the industry must foster a culture that values collaboration over competition, as women in wealth management tend to excel in relationship-building and collaborative environments.

10.7 The Role of AI and Technology

10.7.1 AI as a Game-Changer for the Wealth Management Industry

Artificial intelligence (AI) is increasingly becoming a game-changer in the wealth management industry, with advancements in machine learning, robo-advisors, and data analytics transforming how financial advice is delivered. AI's ability to analyze vast amounts of data, predict market trends, and provide personalized financial recommendations has revolutionized the industry.

For female wealth managers, AI offers a significant opportunity to level the playing field. By automating routine tasks, such as portfolio management and compliance, female wealth managers can focus more on building relationships and providing personalized advice to clients. Furthermore, AI can help women in wealth management better understand and cater to the unique needs of female investors, offering more tailored advice and improving the overall client experience.

10.7.2 How AI Can Empower Female Wealth Managers

AI tools also provide female wealth managers with insights into the investment behavior of their clients, enabling them to develop more targeted strategies that align with their clients' preferences for impact, sustainability, and ethical investments. By using AI to analyze client data, wealth managers can provide customized, value-driven solutions that cater to the growing demand for socially responsible investing.

10.8 The Future of Female Wealth Managers

The wealth management industry is at a crossroads. As more women take on leadership roles and manage their own investments, the need for female wealth managers who understand the unique priorities and risk profiles of female clients becomes increasingly evident. Female wealth managers not only bring diversity to the industry but also help redefine investment practices that prioritize long-term sustainability, impact, and ethical considerations. To ensure greater gender equality in wealth management, firms must actively work to eliminate barriers and provide more opportunities for women to rise to leadership roles. AI and technology will undoubtedly play a role in empowering female wealth managers, allowing them to focus on building meaningful client relationships and creating more tailored, value-driven investment strategies.

10.9 Learn or Lose: Why Wealth Management Will Lose if It Does Not Account for 30% Women

The wealth management industry is undergoing a significant transformation, and one of the most critical shifts is the increasing financial empowerment of women. By 2030, it is estimated that women will control $30 trillion of wealth in the U.S. alone (Bishop, 2021). This staggering statistic highlights a critical need for the wealth management industry to adapt to the preferences and needs of female investors, or risk losing out on a massive opportunity. Firms that continue to ignore or undervalue the importance of gender diversity in both their client base and workforce will likely face significant financial consequences.

Women represent a growing share of the wealth management market, and they are fundamentally changing the landscape of investing. Research shows that women have distinct investment behaviors, risk profiles, and financial priorities, and wealth managers who do not take these factors into account will fail to secure the loyalty of this critical demographic.

10.9.1 The Business Case for Female Investors

Women are not only becoming an increasingly significant demographic in terms of wealth control, but they are also influencing the way investments are managed and the types of products they expect from wealth management services. A report by McKinsey & Company (2020) highlights that women in the U.S. already control 40% of the country's wealth, and this number is expected to increase dramatically over the next decade. If wealth management firms fail to tailor their services to meet the unique needs of women, they risk losing this growing market segment to competitors that are more in tune with the preferences and priorities of female investors.

Case Study A prime example of how wealth management firms can fail by not adapting to women investors is seen in the 2019 decision by Goldman Sachs to introduce a fund aimed at targeting the female market. While initially considered a niche opportunity, the fund found greater success when the company broadened its scope to consider gender-focused investing strategies—acknowledging that women bring unique perspectives and needs to their investment strategies. Goldman Sachs has been more successful in capturing female investors by addressing their concerns and focusing on long-term growth and sustainability (Goldman Sachs, 2019).

10.9.2 Why Wealth Management Will Lose if It Does Not Account for Women

Untapped Potential

Women are expected to control $30 trillion of global wealth by 2030 (Bishop, 2021). This is not just about managing the existing wealth, but the fact that women are increasingly becoming decision-makers when it comes to wealth transfer, estate planning, and family businesses. Wealth management firms that fail to address women's growing financial influence may miss out on capturing a significant share of this wealth.

For instance, wealth transfer from one generation to the next is more often controlled by women, and as they inherit wealth, they bring new priorities to the table—values-driven investing, sustainability, and long-term growth. This is a market that cannot be ignored.

Investment Preferences Are Shifting

Research indicates that women prioritize different investment strategies than men, especially when it comes to ethical, sustainable, and impact investments. Studies have shown that women are more likely to invest with a focus on ESG factors—environmental, social, and governance—reflecting a preference for investments that align with their personal values. A 2020 study from Morningstar (2020) found that women are twice as likely as men to consider ESG criteria when making investment decisions. Wealth managers who fail to integrate these values into their portfolios risk losing female clients to firms that provide investment solutions that align with their ethical and social priorities.

Case Study Fidelity Investments, one of the largest investment management firms in the world, has acknowledged that female investors are more inclined to engage in values-based investing. In response, Fidelity launched the *Fidelity Women's Leadership Fund*, which focuses on companies that actively support female leadership and workplace diversity. This fund quickly became one of Fidelity's most popular products among women investors, demonstrating the importance of tailoring offerings to the needs and values of this demographic (Fidelity, 2020).

Women as Key Decision-Makers in Family Wealth

Another reason why wealth management will lose if it doesn't account for women is the significant role women play in financial decision-making within families. Studies show that women are more involved than ever in managing family wealth, whether through direct control of assets or in the capacity of decision-makers for estates and trusts. The *Transamerica Center for Retirement Studies* (2021) found that women are more likely than men to engage in multi-generational wealth transfer conversations, influencing the investment strategies of family wealth.

Wealth managers must recognize that female investors often consider their family's financial well-being and long-term stability when making decisions. For instance, women may prioritize long-term financial security, retirement planning, and legacy building over short-term profits.

Case Study The *Glenmede Trust* has long been a pioneer in catering to women's financial planning needs. They emphasize generational wealth transfer, and have tailored their services specifically to women who wish to ensure that their families will benefit from long-term, sustainable wealth management. By understanding the family-oriented approach of female investors, Glenmede has effectively captured a significant share of the market by focusing on these needs (Glenmede, 2020).

Impact of Gender Parity in Wealth Management Teams

A wealth management firm that lacks gender diversity within its leadership teams is less likely to understand and meet the needs of its female clients. Numerous studies have shown that diversity leads to more innovative and inclusive decision-making, and this is especially true in wealth management. Women bring a different set of perspectives and priorities that can significantly enhance the firm's ability to relate to and serve female investors.

Case Study The *Fidelity Women's Leadership Fund* example also underscores the value of having gender-diverse leadership. The firm recognized that women bring different insights into financial decision-making, which led them to create a fund that focused on promoting female leadership in the corporate world. Such initiatives not only cater to women's values but also demonstrate the benefits of having a gender-diverse leadership team.

10.10 What Wealth Management Firms Need to Do to Succeed

To avoid missing out on the growing influence of female investors, wealth management firms must take proactive steps to cater to this demographic. Here are several strategies that can help firms succeed:

1. **Diverse Leadership**: Ensure that women occupy leadership roles within the firm. Gender-diverse teams are more likely to understand the unique needs of female investors, creating more effective strategies and solutions.
2. **Focus on ESG and Impact Investing**: Female investors are increasingly driven by social responsibility and impact investing. Wealth management firms must offer investment strategies that incorporate ESG criteria and promote sustainable, socially responsible investments.
3. **Tailor Products to Women's Needs**: Women often approach wealth management differently than men, with a focus on risk mitigation, long-term stability, and values-driven investments. Wealth managers must understand these preferences and offer products that align with women's goals.
4. **Engage in Family Wealth Planning**: Women are key decision-makers in family wealth transfer and estate planning. Wealth management firms must offer services that focus on multi-generational wealth planning and ensure that their clients' families' financial futures are secure.
5. **Education and Empowerment**: Wealth management firms should invest in educational initiatives that empower female investors with the knowledge and tools they need to make informed decisions. By helping women understand their financial options, firms can foster long-term loyalty.

10.11 Conclusion

The wealth management industry is on the cusp of a major shift. Women are playing an increasingly pivotal role in financial decision-making, both for their own wealth and for future generations. Wealth management firms that fail to recognize and address the unique needs of female investors will miss out on a significant growth opportunity. By embracing gender diversity, offering tailored investment strategies, and focusing on sustainable and impact-driven investments, firms can position themselves to succeed in the evolving financial landscape.

10.12 Outlook

Research gaps:

1. Effects of Longevity on WM solutions and the contribution WM can make in address the longevity wealth gap
2. Transition of wealth to generations Z and Alpha
3. New role of women play in the forthcoming wealth transfer
4. The underutilized potential of the WM industry
5. Advancement of technology and its impacts on the WM industry
6. Entrance of new players into the industry
7. Opportunities and risks for the concept of banking as a service (Saas model)

References

Bishop, P. (2021). The rise of women investors and their impact on the wealth management industry. Financial Times.

Deloitte. (2017). The investment preferences of women: A shift toward social responsibility. Deloitte Insights.

Ellevest. (2021). *Women's wealth: Building an inclusive future of finance*.

Glenmede. (2020). *Wealth management for women: Securing future generations*.

Goldman Sachs. (2019). Targeting female investors: How gender-based funds are shaping the future of investing.

GIIN. (2020). The role of women in impact investing. Global Impact Investing Network.

Henriksson, R., et al. (2018). Gender and investment preferences: Evidence from the US market. *Journal of Sustainable Finance & Investment*.

Kozlowski, R. (2001, December 6). Women investors more risk averse than men-study. Reuters. https://www.reuters.com/article/idUS25494921/

McKinsey & Company. (2020). *Women in wealth management: The need for gender diversity in financial services*.

Morningstar. (2019). *ESG investing: Why women are leading the charge*.

Transamerica Center for Retirement Studies. (2021). *Gender and generational wealth planning*. Transamerica Institute.

Vanguard. (2020). *Understanding risk preferences in female investors*.

Wicks, C. J. (2020). Women's wealth and impact investing: The rise of female financial advisors. *Wealth Management Magazine*.

Index

K. Wendt, M. Ra (eds.), *Sustainable Wealth Management Revisited*, Sustainable Finance, https://doi.org/10.1007/978-3-032-02530-2

MIX
Papier aus verantwortungsvollen Quellen
Paper from responsible sources
FSC® C105338

If you have any concerns about our products,
you can contact us on
ProductSafety@springernature.com

In case Publisher is established outside the EU,
the EU authorized representative is:
Springer Nature Customer Service Center GmbH
Europaplatz 3, 69115 Heidelberg, Germany

Printed by Libri Plureos GmbH
in Hamburg, Germany